Windows 7 Enterprise Desktop Support Technician

Revised and Expanded Version

Lab Manual

EXECUTIVE EDITOR	John Kane
EDITORIAL PROGRAM ASSISTANT	Jennifer Lartz
DIRECTOR OF SALES	Mitchell Beaton
DIRECTOR OF MARKETING	Chris Ruel
SENIOR PRODUCTION AND MANUFACTURING MANAGER	Micheline Frederick
SENIOR PRODUCTION EDITOR	John Curley

To order books or for customer service, please call 1-800-CALL WILEY (225-5945).

ISBN 978-1-118-13451-1

Printed in the United States of America

10 9 8 7 6 5 4 3 2

BRIEF CONTENTS

CONTENTS

LAB 1
INSTALLING WINDOWS 7

This lab contains the following exercises and activities:

Exercise 1.1 Installing Windows 7 from a DVD

Exercise 1.2 Configuring IP

Exercise 1.3 Joining a Workstation to a Domain

Exercise 1.4 Identifying your System Components

Exercise 1.5 Using Event Viewer

BEFORE YOU BEGIN

The lab environment consists of student workstations connected to a local area network, along with a server that functions as the domain controller for a domain called contoso.com. The computers required for this lab are listed in Table 1-1.

Table 1-1
Computers required for Lab 1

Computer	*Operating System*	*Computer Name*
Server	Windows Server 2008 R2	RWDC*a* where *a* is the class number
Workstation*xx* where *xx* is the student's number	None	NYC-CL*xx* is your student number

> **NOTE** *In a classroom lab or virtual lab environment, there will be one classroom server and the students will have workstations named using consecutive numbers in place of the xx variable.*

In addition to the computers, you will also require the software listed in Table 1-2 to complete Lab 1.

Table 1-2
Software required for Lab 1

Software	***Location***
Windows 7 Enterprise installation files	DVD (provided by instructor)
Lab 1 student worksheet	Lab01_worksheet.rtf (provided by instructor)

Working with Lab Worksheets

Each lab in this manual requires that you answer questions, shoot screen shots, and perform other activities that you will document in a worksheet named for the lab, such as Lab01_worksheet.rtf. Your instructor will provide you with access to the worksheets. It is recommended that you use a USB flash drive to store your worksheets, so you can submit them to your instructor for review. As you perform the exercises in each lab, open the appropriate worksheet file using WordPad, fill in the required information, and save the file to your flash drive.

SCENARIO

Before you can do the other labs, you must first prepare a Windows 7 system. Therefore, the first task is to take a new computer and perform a clean install of Windows 7 from DVD.

After completing this lab, you will be able to:

- Perform a clean installation of Windows 7 from a DVD
- Configure IP to connect to and communicate with the network and the network's Active Directory Domain Services domain
- Join a newly installed workstation to an Active Directory Domain Services domain
- Use the System Information tool to identify components in a system
- Use Event Viewer

Estimated lab time: 80 minutes

Exercise 1.1	Installing Windows 7 from a DVD
Overview	In the following exercise, you install Windows 7 on a workstation, using a standard installation DVD.
Completion time	30 minutes

NOTE	*In a classroom lab environment, each student should install Windows 7 on his or her own workstation, regardless of its current status. This is to ensure a clean working environment for subsequent labs.*

1. Turn on the computer and insert the Windows 7 installation disk into the DVD drive. Users who are using virtual workstations will need to attach an ISO image of the installation disk to the virtual DVD drive. Since each virtual environment is different, you may need to ask your instructor if you do not know how to do this.

2. Press any key to boot from the DVD (if necessary). A progress indicator screen appears as Windows is loading files.

Question 1	*If your computer tries to boot directly from the hard drive without checking the DVD for a bootable DVD, what settings in the BIOS setup program should you check?*

3. The computer switches to the Windows graphical interface and the *Install Windows* page appears, as shown in Figure 1-1.

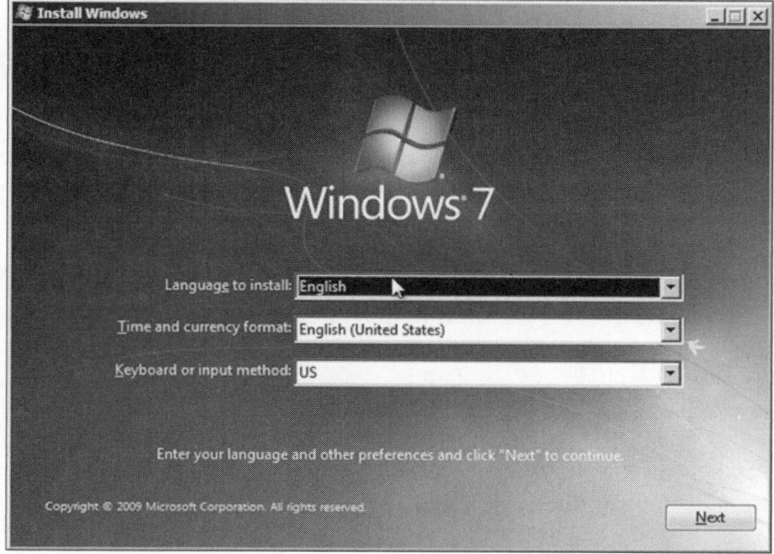

Figure 1-1
The *Install Windows* page

4. Click **Next** to accept the default values for the *Language to install*, *Time and currency format*, and *Keyboard or input method* parameters. The *Install now* screen appears.

5. Click the **Install now** button. The *Please read the license terms* page appears.

6. Select the *I accept the license terms* check box and click **Next**. The *Which type of installation do you want?* page appears.

7. Click the **Custom (advanced)** option. The *Where do you want to install Windows?* page appears, as shown in Figure 1-2.

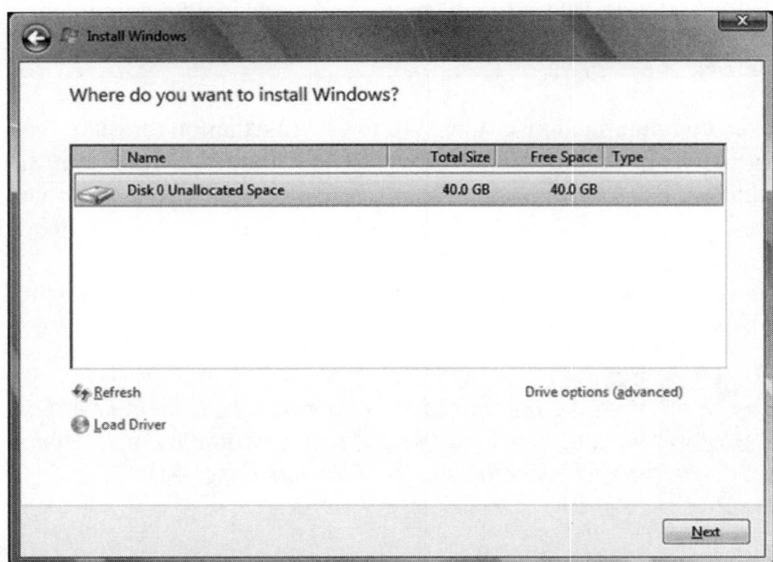

Figure 1-2
The *Where do you want to install Windows?* page

8. Click **Drive options (advanced)**. Additional command buttons for manipulating the drives appear.

9. If the drive already has a partition, select a partition in the list and click **Delete**. A warning box appears, prompting you to confirm that you want to delete the partition.

10. Click **OK**. The system deletes the partition.

11. Repeat steps 9 and 10, if necessary, to delete all other existing partitions on the computer.

12. Click **New**. The new partition controls appear.

13. In the *Size* spin box, specify a size of **40 GB**. This will leave at least 40 GB of unpartitioned space on the computer.

Question 2	*What is the minimum available hard disk space required for the 64-bit version of Windows 7 Enterprise edition?*

14. Click **Apply**. A message box appears, specifying that Windows might have to create additional partitions.

15. Click **OK**. The system creates the partition you defined, as well as a 100 MB partition, as shown in Figure 1-3.

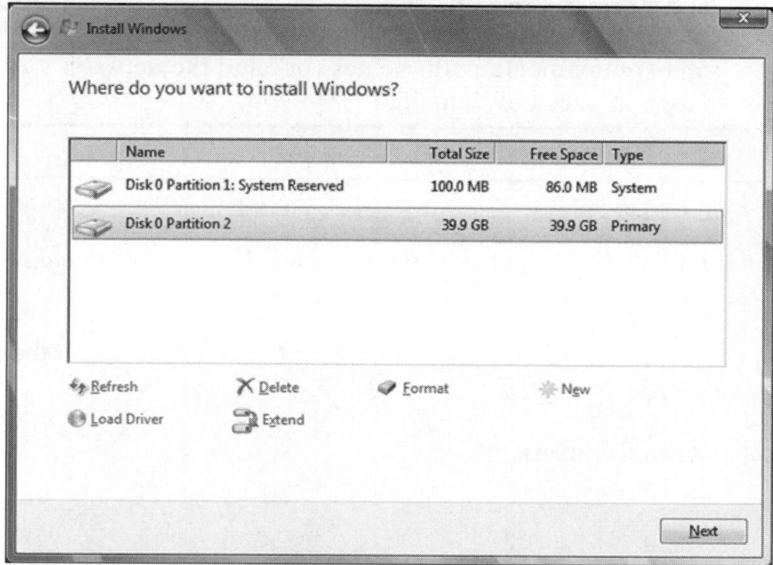

Figure 1-3
New partitions on the *Where do you want to install Windows?* page

16. Select the large partition you just created and click **Next**. The system installs Windows 7, a process that takes several minutes and requires two system restarts. Then, the *Set Up Windows* page appears.

17. In the *Type a user name* text box, type **student**.

18. In the *Type a computer name* text box, type **NYC-CL*xx***, where *xx* is the original number of your workstation, and click **Next**. The *Set a password for your account* page appears.

19. In the three text boxes, type **Pa$$w0rd** and click **Next**. The *Help protect your computer and improve Windows automatically* page appears.

20. Click **Ask me later**. The *Review your time and date settings* page appears. This option will disable Windows updates.

21. From the *Time zone* drop-down list, select the correct time zone or your location. If the date and time specified in the calendar and clock are not accurate, correct the settings and click **Next**. The *Select your computer's current location* page appears.

22. Click **Work network**. The system finalizes your settings and the Windows desktop appears.

23. Remove the Windows 7 installation DVD from the drive.

24. Leave the computer logged on for the next exercise.

Exercise 1.2	Configuring IP
Overview	In the following exercise, you will configure IP so that you connect to and communicate with the network and the network's Active Directory Domain Services domain.
Completion time	10 minutes

1. Click the **Start** button. Then click **Control Panel**. The *Control Panel* window appears.

2. While in *Category* view, click **View network status and tasks** under the *Network and Internet* group.

3. Click **Local Area Connection**.

4. Click **Properties**.

5. Double-click **Internet Protocol Version 4 (TCP/IPv4)**.

6. Select the following IP address and configure the following:

IPv4 Address	10.10.0.1*xx* where *xx* is your student number
Subnet Mask	255.255.255.0
Default Gateway	Leave blank
Preferred DNS Server	10.10.0.2

7. Click the **OK** button to close the *Internet Protocol Version 4 (TCP/IPv4) Properties* box and click **OK** to close the *Local Area Connection Properties*.

8. Click **Close** to click the *Local Area Connection Status* dialog box.

Exercise 1.3	Joining a Workstation to a Domain
Overview	In the following exercise, you join your newly installed Windows 7 workstation to your network's Active Directory Domain Services domain.
Completion time	5 minutes

1. Click **Start**. Then click **Control Panel**. The *Control Panel* window appears.

2. Click *System and Security* > *System*. The System control panel appears.

3. Click **Change settings in the Computer name, domain, and workgroup** section. The *System Properties* sheet appears.

4. Click **Change**. The *Computer Name/Domain Changes* dialog box appears, as shown in Figure 1-4.

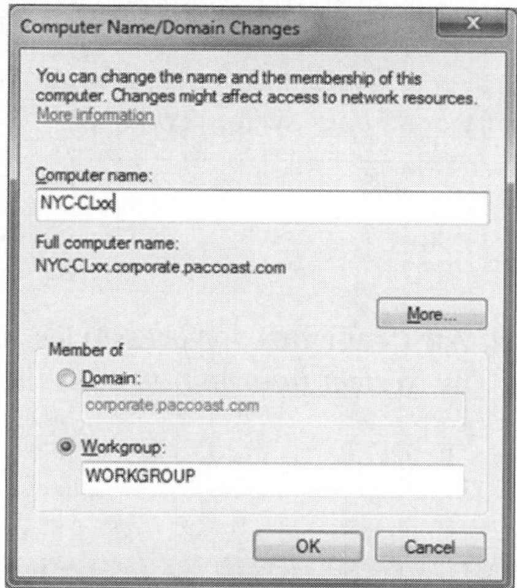

Figure 1-4
The Computer Name/Domain Changes dialog box

5. Select the *Domain* option, and type **contoso** in the text box. Then click **OK**. A *Windows Security* dialog box appears.

6. Authenticate with the user name **Administrator** and the password **Pa$$w0rd** and click **OK**. A message box appears, welcoming you to the domain.

7. Take a screen shot of the message box by pressing **Alt+Prt Scr** and then paste it into your Lab01_worksheet file in the page provided by pressing **Ctrl+V**.

8. Click **OK**. Another message box appears, prompting you to restart the computer.

9. Click **OK**.

10. Click **Close** to close the *System Properties* dialog box.

11. A *You must restart your computer to apply these changes* message box appears.

12. Click **Restart Now**. The computer restarts.

Exercise 1.4	Identifying Your System Components
Overview	The System Information tool enables desktop technicians to quickly look at a machine and determine what is running on the machine. In the following exercise, you will identify your components in your system.
Completion time	15 minutes

1. Turn on the NYC-CL*xx* workstation and log on using the **contoso\Administrator** account and the password **Pa$$w0rd**.

2. Click **Start**. Then right-click **Computer** and select *Properties*.

Question 3	*According to System Properties, what processor and how much memory does your system contain?*

3. Close *System Properties*.

4. Click **Start**. Then click **All Programs > Accessories > System Tools > System Information**. The *System Information* console appears, as shown in Figure 1-5.

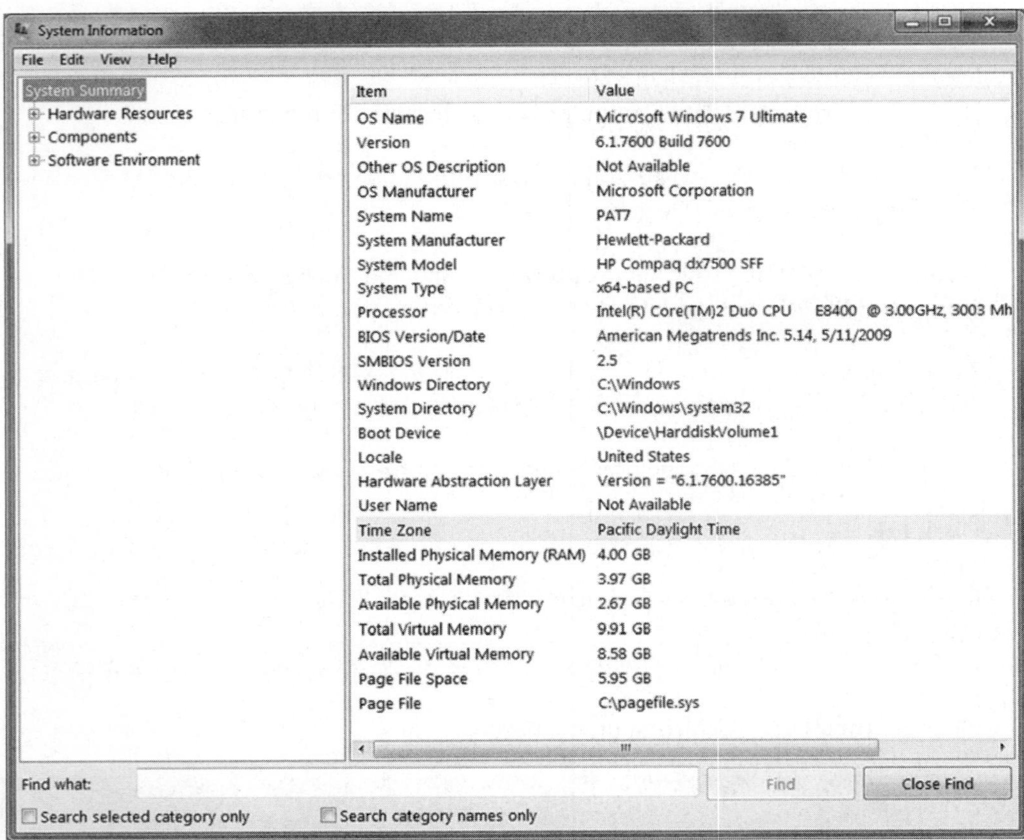

Figure 1-5
System Information console

Question 4	*Record the following:* *What is the System Manufacturer and model?* *How many processors, which processor(s), and at what speed does the processor run?* *How much memory does your system contain?* *What is the version and date of the BIOS?*

5. Expand *Hardware Resources* and click **IRQs**.

Question 5	*What IRQ does the System timer use?*

Question 6	*What IRQ does ATA Channel 0 and ATA Channel 1 use?*

6. Click **DMAs**.

Question 7	*What uses DMA Channel 4?*

7. Click **I/O**.

Question 8	*What I/O address is used by ATA Channel 0?*

8. Expand *Components* and select **Ports**. Expand *Ports*.

Question 9	*How many serial ports does your system have? You can tell by how many name fields are listed.*

9. Expand *Storage* and select **Drives**.

Question 10	*What drives does your system contain?*

10. Select **Disks**.

Question 11	*What disks does your system contain?*

11. Expand *Software Environment* and select **System Drivers**. Look at all the drivers used in your system.
12. Close *System Information*.
13. Physically inspect your system to identify all ports.

Question 12	*Record all ports that your system has including the number of USB ports, 1394 ports, audio ports, serial ports, parallel ports, network jacks, and video ports.*

Exercise 1.5 Using Event Viewer

Overview	In this exercise, you demonstrate some methods for isolating the most important events in the Windows 7 logs. In addition, you will work with a partner to send events from one computer to another.
Completion time	20 minutes

1. Turn on the NYC-CL*a* workstation and log on using the **contoso\Administrator** account and the password **Pa$$w0rd**.
2. Click **Start**. Then click **Administrative Tools > Event Viewer**. If Administrative Tools is not available, open *Control Panel*, select **System and Security**, and then select **Administrative Tools**. The *Event Viewer* console appears, as shown in Figure 1-6.

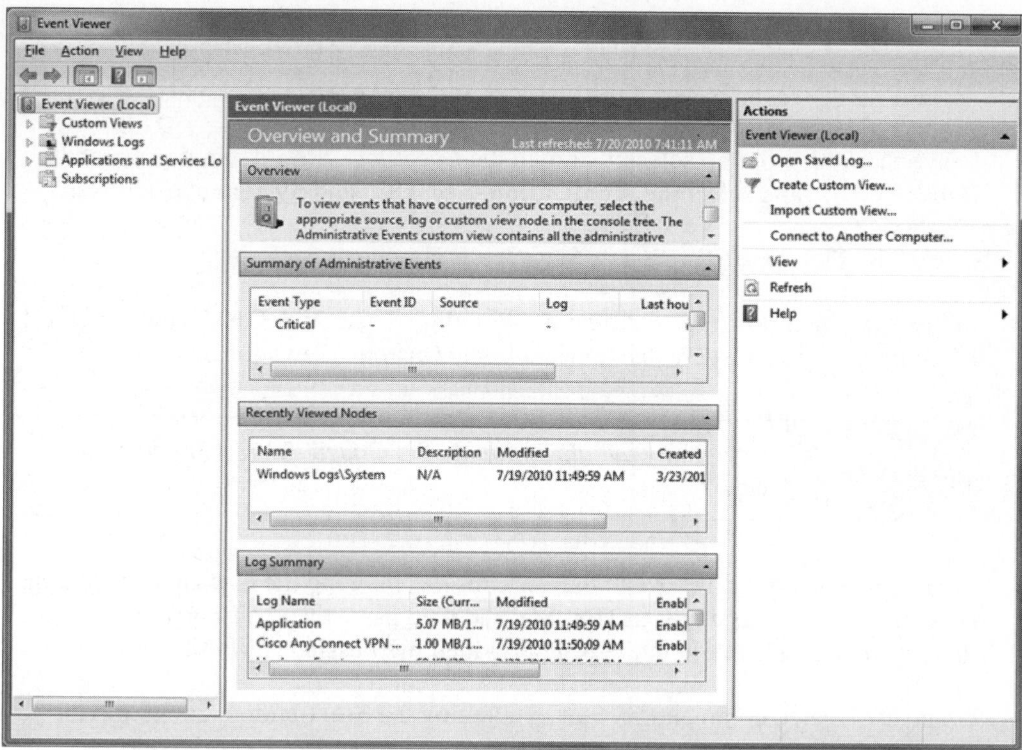

Figure 1-6
The Event Viewer console

3. Expand the *Windows Logs* folder and select the **System log**. The contents of the log appear in the detail pane.

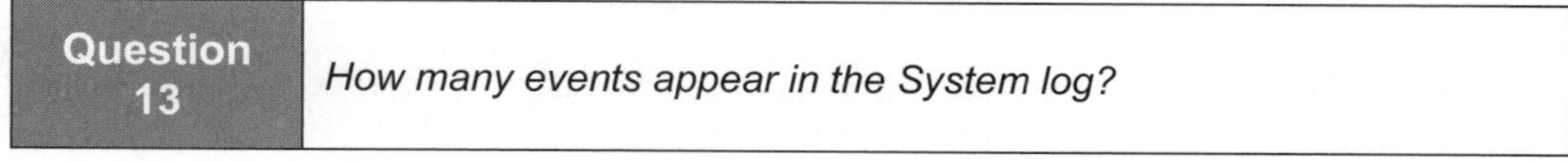

Question 13
How many events appear in the System log?

4. From the *Action* menu, select **Filter Current Log**. The *Filter Current Log* dialog box appears.

5. In the *Event Level* area, select the **Critical and Warning** check boxes. Then click **OK**.

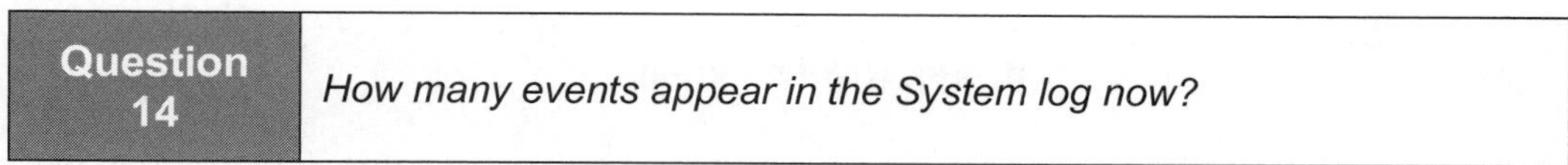

Question 14
How many events appear in the System log now?

6. From the *Action* menu, select **Create Custom View**. The *Create Custom View* dialog box appears.

7. In the *Logged* drop-down list, select **Last 7 days**.

8. In the *Event Level* area, select the **Critical and Warning** check boxes.

9. Leave the *By log* option selected and, in the *Event logs* drop-down list, expand *Windows logs*, and select the **Application**, **Security**, and **System** check boxes.

10. Click **OK**. The *Save Filter to Custom View* dialog box appears.

11. In the *Name* text box, type **Critical & Warning**. Then click **OK**. The *Critical & Warning* view you just created appears in the Custom Views folder.

Question 15	*How many events appear in the Critical & Warning custom view?*

12. Take a screen shot of the Event Viewer console, showing the Critical & Warning custom view, by pressing **Ctrl+Prt Scr** and then paste the resulting image into the Lab01_worksheet file in the page provided by pressing **Ctrl+V**.

13. Open an elevated command prompt by clicking the **Start** button, clicking **All Programs**, clicking **Accessories**, right-clicking **Command Prompt**, and selecting **Run as Administrator**.

14. At the elevated command prompt, as the source computer, execute the following command:

    ```
    winrm quickconfig
    ```

    When it asks you to make the changes, type **Y** and press the **Enter** key.

15. At the elevated command prompt, as the target computer, execute the following command:

    ```
    wecutil qc
    ```

    When it asks you to make the changes, type **Y** and press the **Enter** key.

16. Click the **Start** button, right-click **Computer** and select **Manage**.

17. Expand *Local Users and Computers* and click **Groups**.

18. Double-click the **Event Log Readers** group.

19. Click the **Add** button and add your partner's computer name. Hint: You may need to add *Computer type* to the *Object type*. When the computer name is added, click the **OK** button to close the *Event Log Readers Properties* dialog box.

20. Open the *Event Viewer*, select the *Subscriptions node* and click the **Create Subscription** action in the *Actions* pane.

21. In the *Subscription Properties* dialog box enter the name of your partner's computer.

22. For the *Destination log*, keep **Forwarded Events** selected.

23. Click the **Select Computers** button and click **Add Domain Computers**. Type your partner's computer name and click **OK**.

24. Click the **Test** button. When you have a successful test, click the **OK** button.

25. Click **OK** when finished adding source computers.

26. Click **Select Events**. Then click **Critical**, **Warning**, **Error**, and **Information** and select **Windows logs** for the *Event logs*.

27. Click the **OK** button to close the *Query Filter* and click the **OK** button to close the *Subscription Properties* dialog box.

28. Click the **Edit Opens the Query Filter** dialog box to allow the creation of an event filter to be used for the subscription.

29. Click the **Forwarded Events** to view your partner's events. Note: it may take some time for an event to appear from your partner's computer.

30. Close *Event Viewer*.

LAB 2 CONFIGURING NETWORK CONNECTIONS

This lab contains the following exercises and activities:

Exercise 2.1	Troubleshooting Network Connectivity
Exercise 2.2	Configuring IPv6
Exercise 2.3	Troubleshooting Name Resolution Problems
Exercise 2.4	Looking at Network Statistics and Port Usage
Lab Challenge	Configure Network Card Settings

BEFORE YOU BEGIN

The lab environment consists of student workstations connected to a local area network, along with a server that functions as the domain controller for a domain called contoso.com. The computers required for this lab are listed in Table 2-1.

Table 2-1
Computers required for Lab 2

Computer	*Operating System*	*Computer Name*
Server	Windows Server 2008 R2	RWDC01
Workstation*xx* where *xx* is the student's number	Windows 7 Enterprise	NYC-CL*xx* where *xx* is your student number
Workstation*yy* where *yy* is your partner's student number or your second computer number	Windows 7 Enterprise	NYC-CL*yy* where *yy* is your partner's student number or your second computer number

NOTE

In a classroom lab environment, there will be one classroom server and the students will have workstations named using consecutive numbers in place of the xx *and* yy *variables. In a virtual lab environment, each student will have three virtual machines, named RWDC01, NYC-CL01, and NYC-CL02.*

In addition to the computers, you will also require the software listed in Table 2-2 to complete Lab 2.

Table 2-2
Software required for Lab 2

Software	*Location*
Lab 2 student worksheet	Lab02_worksheet.rtf (provided by instructor)

Working with Lab Worksheets

Each lab in this manual requires that you answer questions, make screen shots, and perform other activities that you will document on a worksheet named for the lab, such as Lab02_worksheet.rtf. Your instructor will provide you with access to the worksheets. It is recommended that you use a USB flash drive to store your worksheets, so you can submit them to your instructor for review. As you perform the exercises in each lab, open the appropriate worksheet file using WordPad, fill in the required information, and save the file to your flash drive.

SCENARIO

You are a Windows 7 technical specialist for Contoso Ltd. a company with workstations in a variety of different environments. You are setting up a testing lab and you are trying to get a better feel for troubleshooting TCP/IP problems. Therefore, you are going build the lab network using Windows 7 computers borrowed from the production network.

After completing this lab, you will be able to:

- Manually configure the Windows 7 TCP/IP client
- Troubleshoot common network connection problems

Estimated lab time: 60 minutes

Exercise 2.1	Troubleshooting Network Connectivity
Overview	Because the lab network you are constructing for Contoso Ltd. must be isolated from the production network, you do not want the lab computers to obtain their TCP/IP settings from the DHCP servers on the production network. Therefore, you must configure the TCP/IP client to use static IP addresses. In addition, you will be working with a partner where one of you is assigned a student number that is an odd number while the other is assigned a student number that is an even number.
Completion time	20 minutes

1. Turn on the NYC-CL*xx* workstation and log on using the **contoso\Administrator** account and the password **Pa$$w0rd**.
2. Open the *Network and Sharing Center*.
3. Click **Local Area connection**.
4. Click the **Details** buttons. Notice the information there, including how long it has been up, the speed of the link, and if it has IPv4 or IPv6 connectivity.
5. Close the *Network Connections Details* dialog box.
6. Click **Start**. Then click **All Programs** > **Accessories** > **Command Prompt**. A *Command Prompt* window appears.
7. In the *Command Prompt* window, type **ipconfig /all** and press **Enter**.
8. Using the information in the Ipconfig.exe display, note your workstation's current TCP/IP configuration settings in Table 2-3.

Table 2-3

TCP/IP Setting	***Value***
IPv4 address	
Subnet mask	
Default gateway	
DNS servers	

Question 1	*How did the computer obtain these settings? How can you determine this?*

Question 2	*If you have an address handed out by a DHCP server and it appears to be the wrong IP configuration, what are the two things you should check?*

9. In the *Command Prompt* window, type **ipconfig /release** and press **Enter**.

10. In the *Network And Sharing Center* control panel, click **Change adapter settings**. The *Network Connections* window appears.

11. Right-click the **Local Area Connection** icon and, from the context menu, select **Properties**. The *Local Area Connection Properties* sheet appears.

12. Select **Internet Protocol Version 4 (TCP/IPv4)** from the components list and click **Properties**. The *Internet Protocol Version 4 (TCP/IPv4) Properties* sheet appears, as shown in Figure 2-1.

13. Select **Use the following IP address**.

14. If your student number is an odd number, change the address from 192.168.1.*xx* where *xx* is your student number. If your student number is an even number, change the address from 192.168.1.2*xx* where *xx* is your student number.

15. In the *Subnet Mask* text box, type **`255.255.255.0`**.

16. In the *Preferred DNS Server* text box, type the DNS Server value from the table.

17. Take a screen shot of the Internet Protocol Version 4 (TCP/IPv4) Properties sheet by pressing **Alt+Prt Scr**, and then paste the resulting image into the lab02_worksheet file in the page provided by pressing **Ctrl+V**.

18. Click **OK** to close the *Internet Protocol Version 4 (TCP/IPv4) Properties* sheet.

19. Click **OK** to close the *Local Area Connection Properties* sheet.

20. In the Command Prompt window, run the **`ipconfig /all`** command again.

Question 3	*When troubleshooting any network connectivity problem, what command should you execute first in determining the problem?*

Question 4	*What command should you use to verify that your TCP/IP stack is running properly?*

Question 5	*What command would you use to test network connectivity with your partner's computer?*

Question 6	*If you ping your partner's computer by IP address, what does this tell you about your network connectivity and what does it* not *tell you about your network connectivity?*

21. Ping your partner's computer by IP address.

Question 7	*Were you able to ping your partner's computer? If not, why could you* not *ping the computer?*

22. Ping your partner's computer by name.

Question 8	*Were you able to ping your partner's computer? If not, why could you* not *ping the computer?*

Question 9	*Can you ping your DNS server? If not, why could you* not *ping the DNS server?*

Question 10	*So if you could not access a DNS server, how were you able to resolve your partner's computer address when you pinged it by name?*

Question 11	*If you are trying to verify network connectivity with a computer on a remote host what is the next logical command to test network connectivity that you should execute?*

23. Change your subnet mask to **255.255.255.240**.

Question 12	*Can you ping your partner's computer? If not, why not?*

Question 13	*Can you ping any other computers in the classroom?*

24. Disconnect the network cable from your computer, either physically or virtually as appropriate.

Question 14	*What information does the ipconfig show?*

25. Reconnect the network cable to your computer.

26. Change your IP configuration back to the original settings that you recorded at the beginning of this lesson for IP address, subnet mask, and primary DNS server.

27. To use the network troubleshooter for a connection, click **Change adapter settings** in the *Network and Sharing Center* to open the *Network Connections* windows, right-click **Local Area Connections** in the *Network Connections* dialog box, and then select **Diagnose**.

28. When the troubleshooter cannot identify any problems, click the **Close the troubleshooter** option.

Question 15	*Your network card most likely has two LEDs. What does each LED show?*

Exercise 2.2	Configuring IPv6
Overview	Because IPv6 will grow in popularity and eventually replace IPv4, you need to know how to configure IPv6 settings.
Completion time	10 minutes

1. Turn on the NYC-CL*xx* workstation and log on using the **contoso\Administrator** account and the password **Pa$$w0rd**.

2. Right-click the **network notification** item in the taskbar to directly launch *Network and Sharing Center*.

3. Click the **Local Area Connection** link.

4. Click the **Properties** button.

5. Click **Internet Protocol Version 6 (TCP/IPv6)** and click the **Properties** button.

6. In the IPv6 text box, select **Use the following IPv6 option** and type the following:

   `2001:0DB8:0000:0000:02AA:00FF:F328:9Cxx`

   where *xx* is your student number.

7. For the *Subnet prefix length*, type **64**.

8. Click the **OK** button to close the *Internet Protocol Version 6 (TCP/IPv6) Properties* dialog box.

9. Click the **Close** button to close the *Local Area Connection Properties* dialog box and click the **Close** button to close the *Local Area Connection Status* dialog box.

10. Open a command prompt and execute the **ipconfig** command.

Question 16	*What is the IPv6 and Link-local IPv6 address?* *IPv6:* ________________ *Link-local IPv6:* ________________

Question 17	*What is the IPv6 and Link-local IPv6 address of your partner's computer in the lab?* *IPv6:* ________________ *Link-local IPv6:* ________________

11. Ping your IPv6 address.

12. Ping your link-local IPv6 address.

13. Ping your partner's IPv6 address.

14. Ping your partner's link-local IPv6 address.

Question 18	*Now that IPv4 and IPv6 are running on the same computer, what option do you need to add to the ping command to ping your partner's computer using IPv4?* *For example, you would use ping 192.168.0.1 /4.*

Exercise 2.3	Troubleshooting Name Resolution Problems
Overview	During this part of the lesson, you will be troubleshooting name resolution problems.
Completion time	10 minutes

1. Turn on the NYC-CL*xx* workstation and log on using the **contoso\Administrator** account and the password **Pa$$w0rd**.

2. Open a command prompt and execute the **ipconfig** command.

Question 19	*What is the address of your computer?*

3. Execute the `ipconfig /all` command.

Question 20	*What is the address of the DNS server?*

Question 21	*If you have an address, 10.10.0.2, what command should you use to determine the name of the computer from the DNS server?*

Question 22	*What is the name of the computer at 10.10.0.2?*

4. Perform a DNS reverse lookup by using the command **nslookup *yourIPAddress***.

Question 23	*What command would you use to determine the address of your partner's computer?*

5. Click the **Start** button, open the *Accessories* folder, right-click **Notepad**, and select **Run as Administrator**.

6. With Notepad, open the *hosts* file in the *C:\WINDOWS\system32\drivers\etc* folder.

7. Add the following entry:

```
192.168.3.1      rwdc01
```

8. Save the host file.

9. Go to the command prompt and **ping rwdc01**.

Question 24	*What address was used for rwdc01?*

10. Execute the following command:

```
nslookup rwdc01
```

Question 25	*So why did the nslookup not use the host file?*

11. Remove the entry in the host file that you added previously and save the host file.

12. Close *Notepad*.

Question 26	*If someone makes a change on the DNS server and you need to clear the DNS cache so that it can get the new setting, what command would you use?*

13. Remove the entry in the host file that you added previously and save the host file.

Question 27	*If you change an IP address, what command would you use to register the new IP address with the DNS server?*

Exercise 2.4 Looking at Network Statistics and Port Usage

Overview	When troubleshooting IP connectivity problems, there are several powerful commands that can show you what is going on with a computer connected to the network.
Completion time	10 minutes

1. Turn on the NYC-CL*xx* workstation and log on using the **contoso\Administrator** account and the password **Pa$$w0rd**.

2. To show the Ethernet parameters, execute the following command:

```
netstat -e
```

3. Run the **`netstat -e`** command again and notice that some the byte count most likely increased for the Received, Sent, or both.

Question 28	*What command would you use to display all connections and ports used?*

Question 29	*What option would you use with the netstat command to display all executables and the listening port associated with those executables?*

4. Run the netstat command that will show all connections and ports used.

5. Execute the following two commands:

   `netstat -r`

   `print route`

Question 30	*Is there an advantage to running either of these commands?*

LAB CHALLENGE: CONFIGURE NETWORK CARD SETTINGS

Completion time	**10 minutes**

From time to time, a network connection does not connect correctly and you have to force the network adapter to use either full duplex or half duplex, or you may need to force it to run at a certain speed such as 10 Mbps, 100 Mbps, or 1000 Mbps. Therefore, what are the exact steps you would have to perform to make these changes?

LAB 3
TROUBLESHOOTING LOGIN PROBLEMS

This lab contains the following exercises and activities:

Exercise 3.1 Troubleshooting Login User Rights

Exercise 3.2 Troubleshooting Disabled and Locked Accounts

Exercise 3.3 Looking at Computer Accounts

Exercise 3.4 Troubleshooting Credential Manager

BEFORE YOU BEGIN

The lab environment consists of student workstations connected to a local area network, along with a server that functions as the domain controller for a domain called contoso.com. The computers required for this lab are listed in Table 3-1.

Table 3-1
Computers required for Lab 3

Computer	***Operating System***	***Computer Name***
Server	Windows Server 2008 R2	RWDC01
Workstation*xx* where *xx* is the student's number	Windows 7 Enterprise	NYC-CL*xx* where *xx* is your student number

NOTE	*In a classroom lab environment, there will be one classroom server and the students will have workstations named using consecutive numbers in place of the xx and yy variables. In a virtual lab environment, each student will have three virtual machines, named RWDC01, NYC-CL01, and NYC-CL02.*

In addition to the computers, you will also require the software listed in Table 3-2 to complete Lab 3.

Table 3-2
Software required for Lab 3

Software	***Location***
Remote Server Administration Tools for Windows 7	\\rwdc01\dowloads\ KB958830-x64-RefereshPkg.msu
Lab 3 student worksheet	Lab03_worksheet.rtf (provided by instructor)

Working with Lab Worksheets

Each lab in this manual requires that you answer questions, make screen shots, and perform other activities that you will document on a worksheet named for the lab, such as Lab03_worksheet.rtf. Your instructor will provide you with access to the worksheets. We recommend that you use a USB flash drive to store your worksheets, so you can submit them to your instructor for review. As you perform the exercises in each lab, open the appropriate worksheet file using WordPad, fill in the required information, and save the file to your flash drive.

SCENARIO

You are a Windows 7 technical specialist for Contoso Ltd. supporting hundreds of Windows 7 computers. Routinely, you receive calls that users are having problems logging in or having authentication problems while accessing network resources.

After completing this lab, you will be able to:

- Resolve user login problems
- Correct disabled and locked accounts
- Reset a computer account
- Work with Credential Manager

Estimated lab time: 60 minutes

Exercise 3.1	Troubleshooting Login User Rights
Overview	When users access a computer or network resource, they will need to be authenticated and authorized. To log in to a Windows computer, you will need to use an account with the correct user privileges. During this exercise, you will be reviewing user privileges that apply to Windows login rights.
Completion time	15 minutes

1. Turn on the NYC-CL*xx* workstation and log on using the **contoso\Administrator** account and the password **Pa$$w0rd**.

2. Click the **Start** button and type **mmc** in the *Search programs and files* text box. Press the **Enter** key. If it asks are you sure that you want to make this change, click **Yes**.

3. Open the *File* menu and select **Add/Remove Snap-in**.

4. Select the **Group Policy Editor** and click the **Add** button. When the *Local Computer* appears, click the **Finish** button.

5. Click the **OK** button to close the *Add or Remove Snap-ins* dialog box.

6. Expand *Local Computer Policy*, *Computer Configuration*, *Windows Settings*, *Security Settings*, *Local Policies*, and *User Rights Assignments*.

7. Scroll down through the list to see how many user rights are assigned to the administrator.

8. Double-click **Allow log on locally**.

Question 1	*What groups are assigned the* Allow log on locally *user right?*

9. Click **Cancel** to close the *Allow log on locally Properties* dialog box.

10. Close the **MMC**. If it asks to save the console settings, click **No**.

11. Open the *Computer Management* console by clicking the **Start** button, right-clicking **Computer**, and selecting **Manage**. Then create a local user called **AdminTest** with the password of **Password01**. Be sure to deselect the *User must change password at next logon* option.

12. Right-click **AdminTest** and select **Properties**.

13. Select **Member Of** and click the **Add** button. Type **Administrators** and click **OK**.

14. Close all windows.

15. Log off as administrator and log in as **NYC-CL*xx*\AdminTest** where *xx* is your student number for your computer.

Question 2	*Why was AdminTest able to log in?*

16. Assuming that your partner also created the AdminTest account, try to log in to your partner's computer with the **NYC-CL*yy*\AdminTest** account using Remote Desktop Connections where *yy* is your partner's computer.

Question 3	*What error message did you get?*

Question 4	*Why could you not log in using remote desktop?*

17. Log in as **Administrator**. Click the **Start** button, right-click **Computer** and select **Properties**. Select **Remote settings**. Select the **Allow connections only from computers running Remote Desktop with Network Level Authentication (more secure)** option. Click the **OK** button to close the *System Properties* dialog box.

18. Assuming your partner has enabled Remote Desktop, try to log in with Remote Desktop Connections on your partner's computer with the **NYC-CL*yy*\AdminTest** account.

Question 5	*What error message did you get now?*

Question 6	*What are the different ways you can fix this problem?*

19. Log in as **Administrator** and add the **AdminTest** account to the Remote Desktop Users.

20. Log out as Administrator.

21. Assuming your partner has enabled Remote Desktop, try to log in with Remote Desktop Connections on your partner's computer with the **NYC-CL*yy*\AdminTest** account.

22. Log in as **Administrator**.

23. Leave the computer logged on for the next exercise.

Exercise 3.2	Troubleshooting Disabled and Locked Accounts
Overview	Account policies are used to protect your user accounts from being easily guessed. Therefore, depending on your domain environment, you will most likely have to deal with disabled and locked user accounts.
Completion time	25 minutes

1. To install the Windows 7 Remote Administrative tools, click **Start**, and in the *Search programs and files* box, type **\\rwdc01\downloads\Windows6.1-KB958830-x64-RefereshPkg.msu** and press **Enter**. A *Windows Update Standalone Installer* message box appears, asking you to install the update for KB958830.

2. Click **Yes**. The *Download and Install Updates* Wizard appears, displaying the *Read these license terms* page.

3. Click **I Accept**. The wizard installs the update, and the *Installation complete* page appears. In addition, the *Windows 7 Remote Administration tools help file* appears.

4. Close the help file window and click **Close** to terminate the wizard.

5. Click the **Start** button and open the **Control Panel**.

6. In Category view, click **Programs** and click **Turn Windows features on or off** in the *Programs and Features* section. Note: It may take a minute or two for the programs to be populated.

7. Expand *Remote Server Administration Tools*. Expand *Feature Administration Tools* and select **Group Policy Management Tools**. Expand *Role Administration Tools* and expand *AD DS and AD LDS Tools*, expand *AD DS Tools* and select **Active Directory Administrative Center** and **AD DS Snap-ins and Command-line Tools**. Click **OK**. It will take a couple minutes to load the Windows features.

8. Close the Control Panel.

9. Click the **Start** button, open **Administrative Tools** and start **Active Directory Users and Computers**.

10. Click the **Start** button and type **mmc** in the *Search programs and files* text box. Press the **Enter** key. If it asks are you sure that you want to make this change, click **Yes**.

11. Open the **File** menu and select **Add/Remove Snap-in**.

12. Select the **Group Policy Object Editor** and click the **Add** button. When the *Local Computer* appears, click the **Finish** button.

13. Click the **OK** button to close the *Add or Remove Snap-ins* dialog box.

14. Expand *Local Computer Policy*, *Computer Configuration*, *Windows Settings*, *Security Settings*, *Account Policies*, and *Password Policy*.

Question 7	*What are the settings for Password Policy?* *Enforce password history:* *Maximum password age:* *Minimum password age:* *Minimum password length:* *Password must meet complexity requirements:*

15. Under *Account Policies*, select **Account Lockout Policy**.

Question 8	*What are the settings for Account Lockout Policy?* *Account lockout duration:* *Account lockout threshold:* *Reset account lockout counter after:*

Question 9	*Can you change the Account Lockout settings. If not, why?*

16. Click the **Start** button, click **Administrative Tools**, and select **Group Policy Management**.

17. Right-click **Group Policy Management** and click **Add Forest**.

18. For the domain name, type **Contoso** and click **OK**.

19. Expand *Forest*, expand *Domains* and expand *constoso.com*.

20. Right-click the **Default Domain Policy** and select **Edit**.

21. Expand *Computer Configuration*, *Policies, Windows Settings*, *Security Settings*, *Account Policies*, and *Account Lockout Policy*.

Question 10	*What are the settings for Account Lockout Policy?* *Account lockout duration:* *Account lockout threshold:* *Reset account lockout counter after:*

22. Click the **Start** button, click **Administrative Tools**, and select **Active Directory Users and Computers**.

23. Expand *contoso.com*.

24. Right-click **Users** and select **New User**. Create a user called **TestUser*xx*** where ***xx*** is your student number. Click the **Next** button.

25. Assign the password of **Password01**. Deselect the *User must change password at next logon* option. Click the **Next** button.

Question 11	*What is the Full Name?* *What is the user logon name?*

26. Right-click the **TestUser*xx*** account and select **Add to a Group**. Type in **Domain Admins** and click **OK**.

27. Log out as Administrator and log in as **NYC-CL*xx*\TestUser*xx*** with the password of **Password01**.

28. Log out as Administrator and log in as **TestUserxx@contoso.com** with the password of **Password01**.

29. Log out as TestUser*xx*.

30. Attempt to log in as **TestUser*xx*** with the password of **password** three times.

31. Attempt to log in as **TestUser*xx*** with the password of **Password01**.

Question 12	*What error message did you get?*

Question 13	*What is the first and most obvious thing you should check when a user is having problems logging in to any computer, application or website?*

32. Log in as **Administrator**.
33. Open **Active Directory Users and Computers**.
34. Right-click **TestUser*xx*** and select **Properties**.
35. Click the **Account** tab. Deselect the *Unlock account* option and click the **OK** button.
36. Log out as Administrator.
37. Log in as **TestUser*xx***.
38. Log out as TestUser*xx*.
39. Log in as **Administrator**.
40. Right-click **TestUser*xx*** and select **Disable Account**.
41. Log out as Administrator and try to log in as **TestUser*xx***.

Question 14	*What error message did you get?*

42. Log in as **Administrator.**
43. Open the **Active Directory Users and Computers**.
44. Right-click the **TestUser*xx*** account and select **Enable Account**.
45. Right-click the **TestUser*xx*** account and select **Properties**.
46. Select the **Account tab** and click **Logon Hours**.
47. Select the current hour and click **Logon Denied**.
48. Click **OK** to close the *Logon Hours* dialog box and click **OK** to close the *TestUser*xx *Properties* dialog box.
49. Log out as Administrator and log in as **TestUser*xx***.

Question 15	*What error message did you get?*

50. Log in as **Administrator**.

51. Open the **Active Directory Users and Computers**.

52. Right-click the **TestUser*xx*** account and select **Properties**.

53. Select the **Account tab** and click **Logon Hours**.

54. Highlight the hour that you restricted before and click **Logon Permitted**.

55. Click **OK** to close the *Logon Hours* dialog box and click **OK** to close the *TestUser*xx *Properties* dialog box.

56. Log in as **Administrator**.

57. Leave the computer logged on for the next exercise.

Exercise 3.3	Looking at Computer Accounts
Overview	To enhance overall security, computers also have accounts within Active Directory. Because of this, you will be asked to troubleshoot them from time to time. During this lab, you will look at how to reset a computer account.
Completion time	10 minutes

1. Open **Active Directory Users and Computers**.

2. Find and right-click your computer. Delete the computer account.

3. Log out as Administrator.

4. Log in as **Administrator**.

Question 16	*What error message did you get?*

5. Log in as **NYC-CL*xx*\administrator** with the correct password for the NYC-CL*xx*\administrator account.

6. Click **Start**. Then click **Control Panel**. The *Control Panel* window appears.

7. Click **System and Security** > **System**. The *System* control panel appears.

8. Click **Change settings**. The *System Properties* sheet appears.

9. Click **Change**. The *Computer Name/Domain Changes* dialog box appears.

10. Select **Workgroup** and type **Workgroup** for the *Workgroup* name. Click the **OK** button.

11. When it gives you a warning saying that you must know the password of the local administrator account, click **OK**.

12. Specify the **Administrator** username and the **Pa$$w0rd** password. Click **OK**.

13. Click **OK** when the *Windows Security* dialog box appears.

14. When the *Welcome to the Workgroup* workgroup appears, click **OK**.

15. When it says to restart your computer, click **OK**.

16. Click the **Change** button again.

17. Select the *Domain* option, and type **contoso** in the text box. Then click **OK**. A *Windows Security* dialog box appears.

18. Authenticate with the user name **Administrator** and the password **Pa$$w0rd** and click **OK**. A message box appears, welcoming you to the domain.

19. Click **OK**. Another message box appears, prompting you to restart the computer.

20. Click **OK**.

21. Click **Close** to close the *System Properties* dialog box.

22. A *You must restart your computer to apply these changes* message box appears.

23. Click **Restart Now**. The computer restarts.

24. Log in as **Administrator**.

25. Open **Active Directory Users and Computers**.

26. Find your computer account and right-click your computer account. Select **Reset Account**. When the account has been successfully reset, click **OK**.

27. Try to log on to the computer again.

Question 17	*What error message did you get?*

28. Once more, log in as a local administrator and add your computer back to the domain again.

29. Leave the computer logged on for the next exercise.

Exercise 3.4 Troubleshooting Credential Manager

Overview	While the local and Active Directory user accounts and passwords are used often within an organization, they are not the only usernames and password used. As a worker with the Contoso Ltd. you have users who need to manage their usernames and passwords.
Completion time	10 minutes

1. Open the **Control Panel**.
2. Click **User Accounts** and then click **Credential Manager**.
3. Click **Add a Windows credential**.
4. Type in your partner's computer name for the *Internet or network address* text box. Then specify User name and password of **contoso\TestUsers*xx*** and the password of **Pa$$w0rd**. Click the **OK** button.
5. Open **Remote Desktop Connection**. Specify the name of your partner's computer in the *Computer* text box. Make sure it is the same name that you specified in the *Credential Manager*. Notice the User name that appears. Click the **Connect** button.

Question 18	*So why did the login fail?*

6. Go back to Credential Manager.
7. If necessary, expand the entry for your partner's computer by clicking the small down arrow button.
8. Click the **Edit** option under your partner's computer entry.
9. Specify the password of **Password01**. Click the **Save** button.
10. Open **Remote Desktop Connection**. Specify the name of your partner's computer in the *Computer* text box. Make sure it is the same name that you specified in the *Credential Manager*. Click the **Connect** button.
11. Log on to your partner's computer. Unfortunately, you will have to log in a second time.

LAB 4
CONFIGURING VPN CONNECTIONS

This lab contains the following exercises and activities:

BEFORE YOU BEGIN

The lab environment consists of student workstations connected to a local area network, along with a server that functions as the domain controller for a domain called contoso.com. The computers required for this lab are listed in Table 4-1.

Table 4-1
Computers required for Lab 4

Computer	***Operating System***	***Computer Name***
Server	Windows Server 2008 R2	RWDC01
Workstation*xx* where *xx* is the student's number	Windows 7 Enterprise	NYC-CL*xx* where *xx* is your student number

> **NOTE**
>
> *In a classroom lab environment, there will be one classroom server and the students will have workstations named using consecutive numbers in place of the* xx *and* yy *variables. In a virtual lab environment, each student will have three virtual machines, named RWDC01, NYC-CL01, and NYC-CL02.*

In addition to the computers, you will also require the software listed in Table 4-2 to complete Lab 4.

Table 4-2
Software required for Lab 4

Software	***Location***
Lab 4 student worksheet	Lab04_worksheet.rtf (provided by instructor)

Working with Lab Worksheets

Each lab in this manual requires that you answer questions, make screen shots, and perform other activities that you will document on a worksheet named for the lab, such as Lab04_worksheet.rtf. Your instructor will provide you with access to the worksheets. It is recommended that you use a USB flash drive to store your worksheets, so you can submit them to your instructor for review. As you perform the exercises in each lab, open the appropriate worksheet file using WordPad, fill in the required information, and save the file to your flash drive.

SCENARIO

Contoso Ltd. is implementing a wireless and virtual private networking (VPN) server. The wireless network will allow users to stay connected while at the corporate offices. The VPN connection will enable users traveling or working from home to connect to the company network through the Internet.

After completing this lab, you will be able to:

- Create a VPN Connection
- Troubleshoot a VPN Connection
- Install a Wireless Connection
- Troubleshoot Wireless Connections

Estimated lab time: 65 minutes

Exercise 4.1	Creating a VPN Connection
Overview	In this exercise, you create a connection that enables the workstation to connect to your RWDC01 server using virtual private networking.
Completion time	10 minutes

1. Turn on the NYC-CL*xx* workstation and log on using the **contoso\Administrator** account and the password **Pa$$w0rd**.

2. Click **Start** and click **Control Panel**. The *Control Panel* window appears.

3. Click **Network and Internet** > **Network and Sharing Center**. The *Network and Sharing Center* control panel appears.

4. Click **Set up a new connection or network**. The *Set Up a Connection or Network* Wizard appears, displaying the *Choose a connection* option page.

5. Select **Connect to a workplace** and click **Next**. The *How do you want to connect?* page appears.

6. Click **Use my Internet connection (VPN)**. The *Do you want to set up an Internet connection before continuing?* page appears.

> **NOTE** *In a classroom lab environment, the* Do you want to set up an Internet connection before continuing? *page does not appear if the network is already connected to the Internet. In a virtual lab environment, the virtual network is not connected to the Internet, but you will bypass the Internet link for the purposes of this lab.*

7. In the *Internet address* text box, type **rwdc01.contoso.com**. In the *Destination name* text box, type **VPN Server Connection**. Select the *Don't connect now; just set it up so I can connect later* option. Select the **Allow other people to use this connection** check box and click **Next**. The *Type your user name and password* page appears.

8. In the *User name* text box, type **Administrator**. In the *Password* text box, type **Pa$$w0rd**. In the *Domain (optional)* text box, type **contoso** and click **Create**. A *The connection is ready to use* page appears, which logs in to the VPN server.

9. Click **Close**.

10. Go back to the *Network Connections* dialog box by clicking the **Change adapter settings** in the *Network and Sharing Center*. Then right-click **VPN Server Connection** and click **Connect**. Finally, click the **Connect** button.

Exercise 4.2 Troubleshooting a VPN Connection

Overview	Now that you have created a VPN connection, you will look at troubleshooting common problems when a VPN connection does not connect or operate properly.
Completion time	25 minutes

1. Click **Network and Internet** > **Network and Sharing Center**. The *Network and Sharing Center* control panel appears.

2. Click **Change Adapter settings** in the left panel.

3. Right-click **Local Area Connection** and select **Properties**.

4. Double-click **Internet Information Version 4 (TCP/IPv4)**.

5. Record the IP address, subnet mask and default gateway.

IP address	
Subnet mask	
Default gateway	

6. Select **Obtain an IP address automatically**.

7. Click **OK** to close the *Internet Protocol Version 4 (TCP/IPv4) Properties* dialog box and click **OK** to close the *Local Area Connection Properties* dialog box.

8. Right-click **VPN Server Connection** and click **Connect**. Type **Administrator** and the **Pa$$w0rd** password. Then click the **Connect** button.

Question 1	*What error appeared?*

Question 2	*So when a user cannot connect to the VPN server using a VPN connection within the corporate network, what is the first thing you should always check when troubleshooting VPN connectivity problems?*

9. Click the **Close** button to close the *Error Connecting to VPN Server Connection.*

10. Open the **Local Area Connection Properties** box again and reset the IP address, subnet mask, and default gateway back to the settings you recorded in step 5.

11. Open a command prompt and try to **ping rwdc01**.

Question 3	*You will not be able to ping many VPN servers because they will have ICMP blocked. Therefore, if you are going to connect to a VPN server over the Internet, what is the first thing you should check on the client's computer that cannot connect to the VPN server?*

12. Right-click **VPN Server Connection** and select **Properties**. Change the *Host Name* to **10.10.0.240**. Click **OK**.

13. Try to connect to the server again.

Question 4	*What error message did you get?*

Question 5	*You just created a VPN connection and you have verified that you have network connectivity/Internet connectivity. However, you still cannot connect to the VPN server (you keep getting error 789) while no one else is having any problems. Therefore, what is most likely the problem?*

14. Close the *Error Connecting* dialog box.

15. Right-click **VPN Server Connection** and select **Properties**. Change the *Host Name* to **RWDC01**.

16. Click the **Security** tab and select **Advanced settings**. Click the **User preshared key for authentication** option. Specify the **Password01**. Click the **OK** button to close *Advanced Properties* and click the **OK** button to close the *VPN Server Connection Properties* dialog box.

17. Right-click **VPN Server Connection** and click **Connect**. Click the **Connect** button.

Question 6	*What error message did you get?*

18. Close the *Error Connecting* dialog box.

19. Right-click **VPN Server Connection** and Select **Properties**. Click the **Security** tab and click the **Advanced Settings** button. Make sure the *Use certificate for authentication* option is selected. Click **OK** to close the *Advanced Properties* dialog box and click **OK** to close the *VPN Server Connection Properties* dialog box.

20. Open **Control Panel**, select **System and Security** and then select **Administrative Tools**.

21. Double-click **Active Directory Users and Computers**.

22. Right-click **constoso.com** and select the **Find** option.

23. Using the **Find Users, Contacts and Groups** dialog box, find **TestUser*xx*** where *xx* is your student that you created in Exercise 3.2 of Lab 3. When you find the user, double-click the **TestUser*xx*** account.

24. Click the **Dial-in** tab. Click the **Deny Access** option in the *Remote Access Permission (dial-in or VPN)* section. Click the **OK** button to close the *TestUser*xx *Properties* dialog box.

25. Right-click **VPN Server Connection** and click **Connect**. Log in with the User Name **TestUser*xx*** with the Password **Password01**. Click the **Connect** button.

Question 7	*So what error message did you get?*

Exercise 4.3	Installing a Wireless Connection
Overview	The Contoso Corporation has many mobile computers running Windows 7. As a Windows technician for the Contoso Corporation, you will need to install and configure wireless connections so that clients can connect to your corporate network.
Completion time	15 minutes

NOTE	*To perform this exercise, you will need to use a laptop or desktop with a wireless network card.*

1. Turn on the NYC-CL*xx* workstation and log on using the **contoso\Administrator** account and the password **Pa$$w0rd**.

2. Click **Start**. Then, click **Control Panel**. The *Control Panel* window appears.

3. Click **Network and Internet** > **Network and Sharing Center**. The *Network and Sharing Center* control panel appears.

4. Click **Change adapter settings**.

5. If the Wireless Network Connection is disabled, right-click the connection and select **Enable**.

Question 8	*When the laptop has a built-in wireless adapter or the wireless adapter is physically installed on a computer and it does not appear in Network Connections, what is most likely the problem if it does show in Network Connections?*

6. Right-click the **Wireless Network Connection** and select **Properties**.

Question 9	*What type of wireless network adapter do you have?*

7. Right-click **Wireless Network Connection** and select **Connect/Disconnect**.

Question 10	*What wireless connections are being broadcasted as available?*

Question 11	*If you are using a laptop computer and you are expecting to see a wireless connection being broadcast but none are being displayed, what should you check first?*

NOTE	*Some OEM mobile computers may also have hot keys or software components that allow you to turn on or off the wireless radio.*

8. Click **Open Network and Sharing Center**.

9. Click **Manage wireless networks**.

10. Click the **Add** button.

11. When it asks you *How do you want to add a network*, click the **Manually create a network profile** option.

12. For the *Network name*, type **Contoso01**. For the *Security type* select **WPA2-Personal**. Type **Pa$$w0rd** for the security key.

Question 12	*By default, what is the Encryption Type used for WPA2?*

13. Deselect **Start this connection automatically** and select **Connect even if the network is not broadcasting**. Click the **Next** button.

14. Click the **Close** button.

15. Go back to **Manage Wireless Networks**. You should notice the Contoso01 connection there.

16. Go back to **Network Connections**, right-click **Wireless Network Connection** and click **Connect/Disconnect**.

17. Click **Contoso01** and click **Connect**.

18. Open a command prompt and execute the **ipconfig** command.

19. Run a command to **ping** the default gateway.

20. Back at the *Network Connections*, right-click **Wireless Network Connection** and click **Status**.

Question 13	*What is the SSID?* *What is the speed?* *What is the signal quality?*

21. Click the **Details** button. Notice that the IPv4 address is the same address that displayed when you executed the ipconfig command.

22. Click **Close** to close the *Wireless Network Connection Status* dialog box.

23. Notice the Wireless connection icon in the taskbar. Click the **wireless connection icon**. Then move the mouse pointer to *Contoso01*, but don't click on it.

Question 14	*What is the Radio Type?*

24. Click **Contoso01** and click **Disconnect**.

Exercise 4.4	Troubleshooting Wireless Connections
Overview	As your company has deployed more and more mobile computers, you are finding that you are troubleshooting wireless connections.
Completion time	15 minutes

NOTE	*To perform this exercise, you will need to use a laptop or desktop with a wireless network card.*

1. Click the wireless connection icon in the taskbar, right-click **Contoso01**, and then click **Properties**.

2. Change the *Network Security key* to **Password01** and click **OK**.

3. Click the **wireless connection icon**, click **Contoso01**, and click **Connect**.

Question 15	*What error message did you get?*

4. Click **Troubleshoot Problems**. After Windows Network Diagnostics attempts to identify the problem, follow the instructions provided by Windows Network Diagnostics. When prompted, click **Detailed Information** to view the *Troubleshooting Report*.

5. Close the Troubleshooting Report.

6. Click the **wireless connection icon**, right-click **Contoso01**, and click **Properties**.

7. Change the *Security type* to **WPA-Personal** and use **Pa$$w0rd** for the *Network security key*.

8. Click the **wireless connection icon**, click **Contoso01**, and click **Connect**. Of course, you receive the same error message.

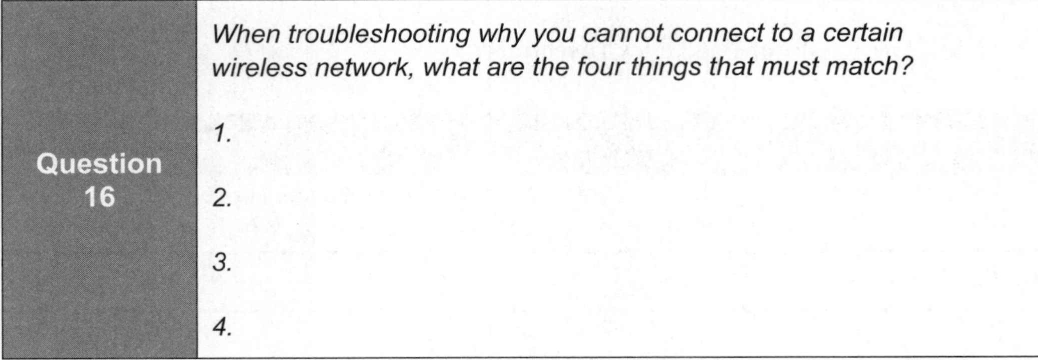

Question 16

When troubleshooting why you cannot connect to a certain wireless network, what are the four things that must match?

1.

2.

3.

4.

9. Change the *Security type* back to **WPA2-Personal**.

10. Confirm that you can connect to the wireless network.

LAB 5
TROUBLESHOOTING HARDWARE ISSUES

This lab contains the following exercises and activities:

Exercise 5.1 Running the Memory Diagnostic Tool

Exercise 5.2 Running Disk Tools

Exercise 5.3 Working with Device Manager

Exercise 5.4 Checking for Unsigned Drivers

Exercise 5.5 Troubleshooting Hardware Problems

BEFORE YOU BEGIN

The lab environment consists of student workstations connected to a local area network, along with a server that functions as the domain controller for a domain called contoso.com. The computers required for this lab are listed in Table 5-1.

Table 5-1
Computers required for Lab 5

Computer	*Operating System*	*Computer Name*
Server	Windows Server 2008 R2	RWDC01
Workstation*xx* where *xx* is the student's number	Windows 7 Enterprise	NYC-CL*xx* where *xx* is your student number

NOTE	*In a classroom lab environment, there will be one classroom server and the students will have workstations named using consecutive numbers in place of the* xx *and* yy *variables. In a virtual lab environment, each student will have three virtual machines, named RWDC01, NYC-CL01, and NYC-CL02.*

In addition to the computers, you will also require the software listed in Table 5-2 to complete Lab 5.

Table 5-2
Software required for Lab 5

Software	***Location***
Lab 5 student worksheet	Lab05_worksheet.rtf (provided by instructor)

Working with Lab Worksheets

Each lab in this manual requires that you answer questions, make screen shots, and perform other activities that you will document on a worksheet named for the lab, such as Lab05_worksheet.rtf. Your instructor will provide you with access to the worksheets. It is recommended that you use a USB flash drive to store your worksheets, so you can submit them to your instructor for review. As you perform the exercises in each lab, open the appropriate worksheet file using WordPad, fill in the required information, and save the file to your flash drive.

SCENARIO

As a desktop technician at Contoso Ltd. you realize that hardware and software are tightly coupled together. Therefore, you need to determine whether problems are specific hardware problems, software problems, or a problem with a driver that allows the hardware to interface with the operating system and applications.

After completing this lab, you will be able to:

- Run the Memory Diagnostic Tool
- Run Disk Tools
- Work with Device Manager
- Check for Unsigned Drivers
- Troubleshoot Hardware Problems

Estimated lab time: 75 minutes

Exercise 5.1	Running the Memory Diagnostic Tool
Overview	You have a computer that is running Windows 7. Unfortunately, the computer has stopped responding several times per day. Since power seems steady, you want to run the memory diagnostic tool.
Completion time	15 minutes

1. Turn on the NYC-CL*xx* workstation and press **F8** before Windows loads. Note: You might need to press F8 repeatedly.
2. When the *Advanced Startup menu* appears, select the **Repair Your Computer** option and press the **Enter** key.
3. When the *System Recovery Options* dialog box appears, click the **Next** button.
4. Specify the **administrator** username and **Pa$$w0rd** password and click **OK**.
5. Click **Windows Memory Diagnostic**.
6. Select the **Restart Now and Check for Problems (Recommended)** option. The computer will automatically reboot and start the memory diagnostic. When the diagnostic tool is completed, it will reboot. The actual diagnostics will take some time to complete.

Exercise 5.2	Running Disk Tools
Overview	Now that the memory checks out okay, you want to check the disks. So you decide to run the disk tools to see if you can find a problem with the disks.
Completion time	20 minutes

1. Turn on the NYC-CL*xx* workstation and log on using the **contoso\Administrator** account and the password **Pa$$w0rd**.
2. Click the **Start** button and Select **Computer**.
3. Right-click the **C** drive and select **Properties**.
4. Click the **Tools** tab.
5. Click the **Check Now** button under *Error-checking*.
6. For sake of time, keep the default settings and click the **Start** button.

7. When a dialog box appears that says *Cannot check the disk while it is in use*, click the **Schedule Disk Check** button.

8. Close all dialog boxes and reboot Windows.

9. When the computer is done and reboots, log on using the **contoso\Administrator** account and the password **Pa$$w0rd**.

10. Click the **Start** button and Select **Computer**.

11. Right-click the **C** drive and select **Properties**.

12. Click the **Tools** tab.

13. Click the **Defragment now** button under *Defragmentation*.

14. Click the **Defragment disk** button.

15. Take a screen shot of the Disk Defragmenter session you created by pressing **Ctrl+Prt Scr**, and then paste the resulting image into the Lab05_worksheet file in the page provided by pressing **Ctrl+V**.

Exercise 5.3	Working with Device Manager
Overview	Since you've installed Windows on this computer, you have never opened Device Manager to see if there are any problems with your drivers. You would also like to see what was detected in your system.
Completion time	10 minutes

1. Turn on the NYC-CL*xx* workstation and log on using the **contoso\Administrator** account and the password **Pa$$w0rd**.

2. Click the **Start** button and select **Devices and Printers**.

Question 1	*What external devices do you have?*

3. Close **Devices and Printers**.

4. Right-click **Computer** and select **Properties**.

5. Click **Device Manager**.

6. Expand *Computer* and notice the drivers assigned to the computer.

7. Expand *Disk Drives*.

Question 2	*What disk drive(s) do you have?*

8. Right-click the drive and select **Properties**.

9. Click the **Volumes** tab.

10. Click the **Populate** button. Notice the logical volumes that appear.

11. Click the **Driver** tab.

Question 3	*Who is the provider and what is the driver date, the driver version, and the digital signer?*

12. Expand *System devices*. Notice all of the drivers.

13. Expand *Network adapters*.

14. Right-click your network adapter and select **Disable**.

Question 4	*What icon appeared for a disabled device?*

15. Right-click your network adapter and select **Enable**.

Exercise 5.4	Checking for Unsigned Drivers
Overview	Microsoft starting using unsigned drivers because third-party drivers were causing many problems. Signed drivers make sure that the driver has been thoroughly tested and includes a digital certificate showing where the driver came from and that it has not been altered. During this scenario, you are going to check for unsigned drivers.
Completion time	10 minutes

1. Click the **Start** button, click **All Programs**, click **Accessories**, right-click **Command prompt** and select **Run as administrator**.

2. At the command prompt, execute the following command:

   `sigverif.exe`

3. Click the **Start** button.

Question 5	*How many unsigned drivers did you find? What are they?*

4. Click the **Close** button to close the *Signature Verification Results* dialog box.

5. Close the i tool.

6. Back at the command prompt, execute the following command:

   `driverquery /si >unsign.txt`

Question 6	*By looking at the command prompt, in what folder is the unsign.txt file created?*

7. Click the **Start** button. Type **`C:\Users\Administrator`** in the *Search programs and files* text box and press the **Enter** key.

8. Double-click the **unsign** file.

9. Scroll through the text file and determine which files are signed and which files are not signed.

10. Close Notepad and the command prompt.

Exercise 5.5	Troubleshooting Hardware Problems
Overview	While this course is focused on configuring and troubleshooting Windows problems, Windows runs on hardware. And from time to time, hardware components fail. Therefore, besides making sure the correct driver is loaded and the correct software components are installed and enabled, you may need to troubleshoot and replace hardware components.
Completion time	20 minutes

NOTE	*Different from the other exercises, this exercise is a paper exercise in troubleshooting computer problems.*

Scenario 1: Computer Will Not Boot

1. You work for the Contoso Corporation. You get a call from a user saying that her computer will not turn on. For most users at your company running Windows 7, the standard computer is an OEM computer with a single dual-core processor, 4 GB of memory, a single network card, a DVD/Blu Ray player, and a Super VGA monitor.

2. Probably before you start troubleshooting, you should introduce yourself and assure the customer that you are there to help. Next you should get information on who the user is and how to contact that person. This may be as simple as getting the user's name, possible email address, and phone number or phone extension.

3. So when talking with the user, you should let the user explain the problem and only ask questions initially for clarification. So up to this point, the user has said she came in as she does every morning and turned the power button to her computer on but nothing happened.

4. One question that is often overlooked that you should ask, "Were any changes made to the system recently, including moving furniture or computers in the office?" While it may or may not be relevant, the answer to the question can save you a lot of time in troubleshooting problems.

Question 7	*So the user has said nothing has happened when she tried to turn the computer on. So far, you have no other information. Therefore, what clarification questions should you ask?*

5. So let's say that the user says that she sees no lights on the computer or display, does not hear the fan run, and did not hear any beeps.

Question 8	*What is the first obvious thing you should have the user check?*

Question 9	*Within the corporation, most computers are plugged into a surge protector. Therefore, what should you also have the user check?*

Question 10	*Can you think of anything that you can have a user check?*

6. At this point, you decided that there is not much more you can do for the user over the phone. So you decide to go pick up her computer. You get to her office and confirm that the computer will not boot and that it is connected properly.

7. When you get back to your cubicle, you connect her computer to your monitor, keyboard and mouse and you confirm that the computer still does not start.

Question 11	*What should your next step be?*

8. You check that all connections and cables are present and connected properly.

Question 12	*If all the connections are connected properly, which item most likely failed if you have no lights and no fan, and the computer provides no beeps and is a high-failure item?*

Question 13	*You made sure that your AC outlet is supplying power and that the power cable is connected properly to the computer and the internal cables are connected properly. Before you replace the power supply, what is an easy item that is overlooked on power supply that may cause the system from not powering on?*

9. So you replace the power supply and everything comes up fine.

Question 14	*If the system still did not work, what are the two primary components that mostly cause the computer not to boot?*

NOTE	*Before you replace the power supply, you could also use a voltmeter or multimeter to measure the output of the power supply.*

Scenario 2: Computer Keeps Rebooting

1. You work for the Contoso Corporation. For most users at your company running Windows 7, the standard computer is an OEM computer with a single dual-core processor, 4 GB of memory, a single network card, a DVD/Blu Ray player, and a Super VGA monitor.

2. A user calls you and says that after turning on the computer, the computer reboots after 15 or 20 minutes. Since the computer is constantly rebooting, the user is not getting much work done.

3. So you ask, "Were any changes made to the system recently?" The user responds no. You also ask when the problems started occurring and if the user has seen any of this before. The user says it started this morning and the user has not seen the problem before.

4. Before you go to his office, what should you instruct that user to try?

Question 15	*When a computer reboots randomly after a certain amount of time, what usually causes this type of behavior?*

Question 16	*Assuming that a component (such as a fan) has not failed, what could you check externally that might cause a system to overheat?*

Question 17	*Before you go to her office, what should you instruct the user to do that might cause this type of problem?*

5. You go to his office and retrieve his computer to take back to your office so that you can troubleshoot the problem.

Question 18	*Before checking for hardware problems, what kind of software problems can cause a computer to reboot randomly?*

Question 19	*When a computer reboots randomly after a certain amount of time, generally, what would cause this type of behavior?*

Question 20	*Before opening the computer, what is the first thing you should check that may cause a computer to overheat?*

6. You then open the computer up. You decide to check all of the connections on the inside of the computer and all looks good.

Question 21	*When first looking inside the computer and even before checking the actual connections, what should you check that might contribute to a system overheating?*

Question 22	*What failure of an internal component would normally cause a system to overheat if it isn't the power supply fan?*

Question 23	*What four main components, if faulty, could cause the system to reboot randomly?*

LAB 6
TROUBLESHOOTING BOOT UP ISSUES

This lab contains the following exercises and activities:

Exercise 6.1 Looking at Safe Mode

Exercise 6.2 Using Last Known Good Configuration

Exercise 6.3 Working with the Boot Environment

BEFORE YOU BEGIN

The lab environment consists of student workstations connected to a local area network, along with a server that functions as the domain controller for a domain called contoso.com. The computers required for this lab are listed in Table 6-1.

Table 6-1
Computers required for Lab 6

Computer	*Operating System*	*Computer Name*
Server	Windows Server 2008 R2	RWDC01
Workstation*xx* where *xx* is the student's number	Windows 7 Enterprise	NYC-CL*xx* where *xx* is your student number

NOTE *In a classroom lab environment, there will be one classroom server and the students will have workstations named using consecutive numbers in place of the* xx *and* yy *variables. In a virtual lab environment, each student will have three virtual machines, named RWDC01, NYC-CL01, and NYC-CL02.*

In addition to the computers, you will also require the software listed in Table 6-2 to complete Lab 6.

Table 6-2
Software required for Lab 6

Software	*Location*
Lab 6 student worksheet	Lab06_worksheet.rtf (provided by instructor)

Working with Lab Worksheets

Each lab in this manual requires that you answer questions, make screen shots, and perform other activities that you will document on a worksheet named for the lab, such as Lab06_worksheet.rtf. Your instructor will provide you with access to the worksheets. It is recommended that you use a USB flash drive to store your worksheets, so you can submit them to your instructor for review. As you perform the exercises in each lab, open the appropriate worksheet file using WordPad, fill in the required information, and save the file to your flash drive.

SCENARIO

You are a desktop technician for Contoso Ltd. You have a computer that is not booting properly. Therefore, you would like to determine what is causing it to fail and run a couple of tools to repair your system.

After completing this lab, you will be able to:

- Start the computer in safe mode
- Use the Last Known Good Configuration to roll back a driver
- Repair components needed for boot up

Estimated lab time: 50 minutes

Exercise 6.1 Looking at Safe Mode

Overview	You want to troubleshoot a program or device driver that is causing your computer not to run properly. Therefore, you want to start the computer in Safe Mode.
Completion time	15 minutes

1. Turn on the NYC-CL*xx* workstation and press **F8** before Windows loads.

2. When the *Advanced Startup* menu appears, select **Safe mode**.

3. Log on using the **contoso\Administrator** account and the password **Pa$$w0rd**. When Windows has completed boot, notice the safe mode labels on all four corners.

4. Try to open Device Manager.

Question 1	*Did Device Manager open?*

5. Try to open System Configuration (msconfig.exe).

Question 2	*Did System Configuration open?*

6. Try to open Internet Explorer and connect to the Microsoft website.

Question 3	*What option should you have selected if you want to have Internet access (including accessing the Microsoft website)?*

7. Reboot the computer once more and press **F8** to access the Advanced Boot menu.

8. Select **Last Known Good Configuration** and boot the computer.

9. Log on using the **contoso\Administrator** account and the password **Pa$$w0rd**.

10. Click the **Start** button and execute the **msconfig** command in the *Search Programs and Files* text box.

11. Select the **Boot** tab.

12. Click the **Advanced options** button.

13. If you have more than one processor, make sure that the *Number of processors* option is selected and the maximum number of processors is selected for your system. Click the **OK** button.

Question 4	*What programs automatically execute during start up.*

14. Close *System Configuration.*

15. Leave the computer logged on for the next exercise.

Exercise 6.2	Using Last Known Good Configuration
Overview	If you load a driver or software package and the computer no longer boots, you can use the Last Known Good Configuration. Therefore, during this exercise, you will load an incompatible driver and use the Last Known Good Configuration to roll back the driver.
Completion time	10 minutes

1. Click the **Start** button, right-click **Computer**, and click **Properties**. Select **Device Manager**.
2. Expand *Keyboards*.
3. Right-click your keyboard and click **Properties**. Click the **Driver** tab.

Question 5	*What driver are you using?*

4. Click the **Update Driver** button.
5. Click **Browse my computer for driver software**.
6. Click **Let me pick from a list of device drivers on my computer**.
7. Uncheck the *Show compatible hardware* check box.
8. Select **Microsoft** as the *manufacturer*, select **Microsoft Keyboard Elite for Bluetooth (106/109)**, and click the **Next** button. If it says that is not recommended, click the **Yes** button to continue.
9. When the driver is installed, click the **Close** button.
10. Click the **Roll Back Driver** button and click **Yes** you want to roll back to the previously installed driver software.

Question 6
What driver shows up now?

11. Click the **Update Driver** button.
12. Click **Browse my computer for driver software**.
13. Click **Let me pick from a list of device drivers on my computer**.
14. Uncheck the *Show compatible hardware* check box.

15. Select **Microsoft** as the *manufacturer*, and select **Microsoft Keyboard Elite for Bluetooth (106/109)**, and click the **Next** button. If it says that is not recommended, click the **Yes** button to continue.

16. When the driver is installed, click the **Close** button.

17. Click **Close** to close the *Keyboard Properties* dialog box. Reboot the computer.

Question 7	*Can you log on?*

18. Reboot once more.

19. As Windows is starting, press **F8** immediately to access the *Advanced Boot Options* menu.

20. When the *Advanced Boot* menu appears, use the keyboard to select **Last Known Good Configuration (advanced)**, and then press the **Enter** key.

21. Log in with the **contoso\administrator** and the password of **Pa$$w0rd**.

22. Open **Device Manager** to verify that you have the original keyboard driver loaded.

23. Leave the computer logged on for the next exercise.

Exercise 6.3	Working with the Boot Environment
Overview	There will be times when certain components that are needed for boot up will become corrupted. Therefore, you will need to learn how to repair these components without reinstalling the system from scratch.
Completion time	25 minutes

1. Click the **Start** button, right-click **Computer**, and click **Properties**.

2. In *System*, click **Advanced system settings**.

3. Click the **Settings** button in the *Startup and Recovery* section.

Question 8	*What is the default operating system, the time to display the operating system, and the time to display recover options?* *Default operating system:* *Time to display operating system:* *Time to display recovery options when needed:*

Question 9	*If a dump is created, where is the dump file created?*

Question 10	*Where is the %systemroot% folder?*

4. Click **OK** to close the *Startup and Recovery* dialog box and click **OK** to close the *System Properties* dialog box.

5. Open an elevated command prompt by clicking the **Start** button, clicking **All Programs**, clicking **Accessories**, right-clicking **Command Prompt**, and clicking **Run as administrator**.

6. Execute the following command:

```
Bcdedit /enum
```

Question 11	*Where is the Windows Boot Manager located?*

Question 12	*Where is the Windows Boot Loader?*

7. At the command prompt, execute the following command

```
Bcdedit /export C:\bcdback
```

8. At the command prompt, execute the following command:

```
Bcdedit /delete {bootmgr} /f
```

9. Shut down and reboot the computer.

Question 13	*What error message did you get?*

10. Insert the Windows installation DVD and reboot the computer again so that you boot from the Windows installation DVD. Press the **space bar** if necessary to boot from the DVD.

11. When prompted to install Windows, click the **Next** button.

12. Instead of clicking the *Install Now* option, click **Repair your computer**.

13. When it displays the *System Recovery Options* dialog box, click the **Repair and restart** button.

14. Make sure Windows starts up properly.

Question 14	*If you had to rebuild the BDC using the bootrec command, what would be the entire command?*

15. Reboot the computer press the **F8** key before Windows starts.

16. When the *Advanced Boot* menu appears, select **Repair your computer**.

17. When the *System Recovery Options* dialog box appears, click the **Next** button.

18. Specify the administration username and password and click **OK**.

19. Select **Startup Repair**.

20. Select **Command Prompt**.

21. After it does the startup repair, select the **Command Prompt**.

22. At the command prompt, run the **bootrec /fixmbr** to repair the master boot record.

23. At the command prompt, run the **bootrec /fixboot** to write a new boot sector onto the system partition or volume.

24. Close the command prompt window.

25. Click the **Restart** button.

LAB 7
RECOVERY FOLDERS AND FILES

This lab contains the following exercises and activities:

Exercise 7.1 Working with Folders

Exercise 7.2 Using Restore Points

Exercise 7.3 Creating a Backup

BEFORE YOU BEGIN

The lab environment consists of student workstations connected to a local area network, along with a server that functions as the domain controller for a domain called contoso.com. The computers required for this lab are listed in Table 7-1.

Table 7-1
Computers required for Lab 7

Computer	*Operating System*	*Computer Name*
Server	Windows Server 2008 R2	RWDC01
Workstation*xx* where *xx* is the student's number	Windows 7 Enterprise	NYC-CL*xx* where *xx* is the student's number
Workstation*yy* where *yy* is the student's number	Windows 7 Enterprise	NYC-CL*yy* where *yy* is the student's number

> **NOTE**
> *In a classroom lab environment, there will be one classroom server and the students will have workstations named using consecutive numbers in place of the* xx *and* yy *variables. In a virtual lab environment, each student will have three virtual machines, named RWDC01, NYC-CL1, and NYC-CL2.*

In addition to the computers, you will also require the software listed in Table 7-2 to complete Lab 7.

Table 7-2
Software required for Lab 7

Software	***Location***
Windows 7 Enterprise installation files	\\rwdc01\downloads\win7ent
Lab 7 student worksheet	Lab07_worksheet.rtf (provided by instructor)

Working with Lab Worksheets

Each lab in this manual requires that you answer questions, make screen shots, and perform other activities that you will document on a worksheet named for the lab, such as Lab07_worksheet.rtf. Your instructor will provide you with access to the worksheets. It is recommended that you use a USB flash drive to store your worksheets, so you can submit them to your instructor for review. As you perform the exercises in each lab, open the appropriate worksheet file using WordPad, fill in the required information, and save the file to your flash drive.

SCENARIO

You are a Windows 7 technical specialist for Contoso Ltd. a company with workstations in a variety of different environments. You are currently assigned to the desktop support help desk and, as a result, you are faced with a number of problems concerning file sharing and access control.

After completing this lab, you will be able to:

- Configure NTFS and share permissions
- Use restore points
- Restore files from backups

Estimated lab time: 55 minutes

Exercise 7.1	Working with Folders
Overview	For the Contoso Corporation, you have a user who created a data folder that only he can access. Your task is to open up the folder so that others can access it. Therefore, during this exercise, you will take ownership of the folder and reset the permissions.
Completion time	25 minutes

1. Turn on the NYC-CL*xx* workstation and log on using the **contoso\Administrator** account and the password **Pa$$w0rd**.
2. Click the **Start** button, right-click **Computer** and select **Manage**.
3. Expand *Local Users and Groups* and click **Users**.
4. Right-click **Users** and click **New User**.
5. For the *User name* and *Full name* text boxes, type **TestUser**.
6. For the *password*, type **Password01**.
7. Deselect the *User must change password at next logon* and click the **Create** button.
8. Click the **Close** button to close the *New User* dialog box.
9. Right-click the **new user** and select **Properties**.
10. Click the **Member of** tab and add the local *Administrators* group. Click **OK** to close the *TestUser Properties* dialog box.
11. Log out as administrator and log in as **TestUser**.
12. Click the **Start** button and click **Computer**.
13. Double-click the **Local Disk (C:)** Drive.
14. Right-click the **Local Disk (C:)** drive to create a new folder named *TestData*.
15. Right-click the **TestData** folder and select **Properties**.
16. Click the **Sharing** tab.
17. Click the **Advanced Sharing** button.
18. Click the **Share this folder** option.
19. Click **OK** to close the *Advanced Sharing* dialog box.

20. Click the **Security** tab.

21. Click the **Advanced** button.

22. Click the **Change Permissions** button.

23. Deselect the *Include inheritable permissions from this object's parent*. When it asks if you want to proceed, click the **Remove** button.

24. Click the **Add** button. Change the location to the *local computer* and add *TestUser*. Click **OK** to close the *Select User or Group* dialog box.

25. Click the **Allow Full** button permission and click **OK**.

26. Click **OK** to close the *Advanced Security Settings* for TestData.

27. Click **OK** to close the *TestData Properties* dialog box.

28. Open the **TestData** folder.

29. Right-click the **white part of the folder** and click **New**. Select **Text Document**. Type **Test Document** and press the **Enter** key.

30. Open the **text document** and type **your name**. Save and close the text document.

31. Log out as TestUser and login as **Administrator**.

32. Click the **Start** button, type **your_computer_name** in the *Search programs and files* text box, and press the **Enter** key.

33. Double-click **TestData**.

Question 1	*What error message did you get?*

34. Click the **Start** button and click **Computer**. Double-click the **C drive**. Double-click **TestData**.

Question 2	*What error message did you get?*

35. Click **Continue** to permanently get access to this folder.

Question 3	*What error did you get now?*

36. Click the **Close** button.

37. To be able to access this folder, you are going to have to reset the permissions by first taking ownership. Unfortunately, to efficiently take ownership of that folder and all objects in the folder, it easier to first shut off UAC (assuming it is still on). Therefore, click the **Start** button and open the **Control Panel**.

38. Click **Users Accounts**, and then click **User Accounts** again. Click **Change User Account Control Settings**. Move the slide to the bottom and click **Yes**. When it asks if you want changes to occur, click **Yes**.

39. Click the **Start** button, click **Computer** and then open the **Local Disk (C:)** drive.

40. Right-click the **TestData** folder and click **Properties**. Then click the **Security** tab.

41. When you get the message saying you must be an administrative user with permissions to view this document, click the **Continue** button.

42. Click the **Advanced** button and select the **Owner** tab. Click the **Edit** button and select **Administrators**. Select the **Replace owner on subcontainers and objects**. Click **OK**. Click **OK** to close the *Windows Security* dialog box.

43. Click **OK** to close the *Advanced Security Settings* for TestData dialog box and click **OK** to close the **TestData Properties** dialog box. If it asks to continue, click **Yes**.

44. Double-click **TestData** to open the folder.

45. Double-click the **Test Document** to make sure you can open it.

46. Add today's date to the text file. Then save the document and close it.

47. Go back to the root directory of the C drive.

48. Right-click **TestData** and select **Properties**. Click the **Security** tab. Click the **Advanced** button. Click the **Change Permissions** button. Select the *Include inheritable permissions from this object's parent* and *Replace all child object permissions with inheritable permissions from this object* options.

49. Click **OK** to close the *Advanced Security Settings* for TestData. Click **Yes** to continue. Click **OK** to close the *Advanced Security Settings* for TestData. Click **OK** to close the *TestData Properties* dialog box.

50. Double-click the **TestData** folder.

51. Right-click the **Test Document** and select **Properties**. Click the **Security** tab.

Question 4	*What groups or users have access to the Test Document text file?*

52. Close the *Properties* dialog box.

53. Click the **Start** button, type **\\your_computer_name** in the *Search programs and files* text box, and press the **Enter** key.

54. Double-click the **TestData** folder.

55. Double-click the **Test Document**.

56. Add the day of the week to the document. Try to save the document.

Question 5	*What error message did you get?*

Question 6	*What is the problem?*

57. Click **OK** to close the *Access is denied* message.

58. Close the *Test Document* without saving the document.

59. Go back to the root directory of the C drive.

60. Right-click the **TestData** folder and select **Properties**.

61. Click the **Sharing** tab. Click the **Advanced Sharing** button. Click the **Permissions** button.

62. With *Everyone* selected, click **Allow Full Control** and click **OK**.

63. Click **OK** to close the *Advanced Sharing* dialog box and click **OK** to close the *TestData Permissions* dialog box.

64. Go back to the *\\your_computer_name\TestData* folder.

65. Open the **Test Document** text file. Add the day of the week. Save the changes and close notepad.

66. Close all of the folders.

67. Open the **Control Panel**. Click **User Accounts** and click **User Accounts**. Click **Change User Account Control Settings**. Slide the slider to the second-highest setting, which is the default setting. Click **OK** to close the *User Account Control Settings*.

68. Restart Windows.

Exercise 7.2	Using Restore Points
Overview	Restore points are created often when you install software or make significant changes. You can also create restore points manually at any time. If you make a change or install software that makes Windows not work properly, you can try to go back to a previous restore point.
Completion time	15 minutes

1. Log in as **Administrator**.
2. Click the **Start** button, right-click **Computer** and select **Properties**.
3. Click **System Protection**.

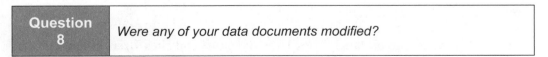

Question 7	*Is the Protection enabled for the C drive?*

4. To create a Restore Point, click the **Create** button.
5. For the description, type **Test Restore Point** and click the **Create** button.
6. When the restore point is created successfully, click the **Close** button.
7. Click the **System Restore** button on the *System Protection* tab.
8. Click the **Choose a different restore point** option and click the **Next** button.
9. Select the **Test Restore Point** and click the **Next** button.
10. Click the **Finish** button.
11. When it asks you to continue, click the **Yes** button. The Restore may take several minutes.
12. Log in as **Administrator**.

Question 8	*Were any of your data documents modified?*

13. Click **Close** to close the *System Restore* dialog box.

Exercise 7.3	Creating a Backup
Overview	To enable network users to access the files in Luz's shared folders, they must have the appropriate NTFS permissions. In this exercise, you configure the permissions to enable the guest user to access the shared folder.
Completion time	15 minutes

1. Click the **Start** button, right-click **Computer** and select **Manage**.
2. Under *Storage*, select **Disk Management**.
3. Right-click the **free space** on your disks and click **New Simple volume**.
4. When the wizard starts, click the **Next** button.
5. When it asks for the Volume size, click the **Next** button.
6. When it asks to assign a drive letter, select the **X** drive. Click the **Next** button.
7. When it is ready to format the volume, click the **Next** button.
8. When the wizard is complete, click the **Finish** button.
9. On the *C* drive, create a **Data** folder.
10. Open the *Data* folder.
11. Right-click the **empty space** of the *Data* folder and select **New**, then **Text Document** and press **Enter**.
12. Click **Start**, click **Add Programs**, select **Maintenance**, and click **Backup and Restore**.
13. Click the **Set up backup** option.
14. When it asks you for the destination, click the **X** drive. Click the **Next** button.
15. Click the **Let me choose** option and click the **Next** button.
16. When it asks what to backup, deselect all options including *the include a system image of drives* option. Expand the *C* drive and select the **Data** folder. Click the **Next** button.
17. Click the **Save settings and run backup** button.
18. When the backup is complete, go back to the *Data* folder and delete the text file.
19. Go back to the *Backup and Restore* program and click **Restore my files**.

20. Click the **Browse for files** button.

21. Double-click the **Backup of C:** folder, double-click the **Data** folder and select the text document. Click the **Add files** button. Click the **Next** button.

22. When it asks where to restore the file, click the **Restore** button.

23. Take a screen shot confirming that the file was restored by pressing **Alt+Prt Scr**, and then paste the resulting image into the Lab07_worksheet file in the page provided by pressing **Ctrl+V**.

24. When the file has been restored, click the **Finish** button.

LAB 8
WORKING WITH PRINTERS

This lab contains the following exercises and activities:

BEFORE YOU BEGIN

The lab environment consists of student workstations connected to a local area network, along with a server that functions as the domain controller for a domain called contoso.com. The computers required for this lab are listed in Table 8-1.

Table 8-1
Computers required for Lab 8

Computer	***Operating System***	***Computer Name***
Server	Windows Server 2008 R2	RWDC01
Workstation*xx* where *xx* is the student's number	Windows 7 Enterprise	NYC-CL*xx* where *xx* is the student's number

NOTE	*In a classroom lab environment, there will be one classroom server and the students will have workstations named using consecutive numbers in place of the* xx *and* yy *variables. In a virtual lab environment, each student will have three virtual machines, named RWDC01, NYC-CL1, and NYC-CL2.*

In addition to the computers, you will also require the software listed in Table 8-2 to complete Lab 8.

Table 8-2
Software required for Lab 8

Software	***Location***
Lab 8 student worksheet	Lab08_worksheet.rtf (provided by instructor)

Working with Lab Worksheets

Each lab in this manual requires that you answer questions, shoot screen shots, and perform other activities that you will document in a worksheet named for the lab, such as Lab08_worksheet.rtf. Your instructor will provide you with access to the worksheets. It is recommended that you use a USB flash drive to store your worksheets, so you can submit them to your instructor for review. As you perform the exercises in each lab, open the appropriate worksheet file using WordPad, fill in the required information, and save the file to your flash drive.

SCENARIO

You are a Windows 7 technical specialist for Contoso Ltd. a company with workstations in a variety of different environments. You have been assigned the task of installing some new printers and troubleshooting several printers that have already been installed.

After completing this lab, you will be able to:

- Install and configure a local printer
- Install and configure a network printer
- Troubleshoot common printer problems

Estimated lab time: 60 minutes

Exercise 8.1	Installing a Local Printer
Overview	The Contoso Corporation purchased some personal laser printers that need to be installed for some executives in the company. Therefore, you will need to go several offices and install these local printers. In addition, you will need to share the printers so that they can be accessed by the executive assistant.
Completion time	10 minutes

1. Turn on the NYC-CL*xx* workstation and log on using the **contoso\Administrator** account and the password **Pa$$w0rd**.

2. Click **Start** and then click **Control Panel**. The *Control Panel* window appears.

3. Click **Hardware and Sound > Devices and Printers**. The *Devices and Printers* control panel appears.

Question 1	*What printer is already there?*

4. Click **Add a printer**. The *Add Printer Wizard* appears, displaying the *What type of printer do you want to install?* page.

5. Click **Add a local printer**. The *Choose a printer port* page appears.

6. Leaving the *Use an existing port* option selected, select **LPT2: (Printer Port)** from the drop-down list and click **Next**. The *Install the printer driver* page appears.

7. In the *Manufacturer* column, select **HP**. In the *Printers* column, select **HP LaserJet 5200 Series PCL 5** and click **Next**. The *Type a printer name* page appears.

8. In the *Printer Name* text box, type **HPLJ5200** and click **Next**. The wizard installs the driver and the *Printer Sharing* page appears.

9. Click **Finish**. The *HPLJ5200* icon appears in the *Devices and Printers* control panel.

10. In the *Devices and Printers* control panel, right-click the **HPLJ5200 printer icon** and, from the context menu, select **Printer properties**. The *HPLJ5200 Properties* sheet appears.

11. Click the **Sharing** tab.

12. Select the **Share this printer** check box. Leave the *Render print jobs on client computers* check box selected, and select the **List in the directory** check box. Then click **OK**.

Exercise 8.2	Installing a Network Printer
Overview	The Contoso Corporation also purchased and installed a new centralized printer to be used by multiple computers. You need to go around to the various computers and add the central printer to some users and to add some local shared printers to others.
Completion time	15 minutes

1. In the *Devices and Printers* control panel, click the **Add a printer** button.

2. Click **Add a network, wireless or Bluetooth printer,** then click **The printer that I want isn't listed**.

3. Select **add a printer using a TCP/IP address or hostname**.

4. Under *Device* type, select **TCP/IP Device**. Then type **10.10.0.241** in the *Hostname or IP address* text box.

Question 2	*What is the port name?*

5. Deselect the *Query the printer and automatically select the driver to use* option and click the **Next** button. It will take a minute or two while it attempts to contact the printer.

6. On the *Additional Port information required* area, make sure **Standard/Generic Network Card** is selected and click the **Next** button.

7. Select **HP** for the *manufacturer* and **HP LaserJet 5200 Series PCL 5** for *Printers* and click the **Next** button.

8. When it says that a driver is already installed, select the **Use the driver that is currently installed (recommended)** option and click the **Next** button.

9. For the *Printer name*, type **Network HPLJ5200** and click the **Next** button.

10. Click **Finish**. The *Network HPLJ5200 icon* appears in the *Devices and Printers* control panel.

11. In the *Devices and Printers* control panel, right-click the **Network HPLJ5200 printer icon** and, from the context menu, select **Printer properties**. The *HPLJ5200 Properties* sheet appears.

Question 3	*What port does the standard TCP/IP use?*

12. Click the **Sharing** tab.

13. Select the **Share this printer** check box. Leave the *Render print jobs on client computers* check box selected, and select the **List in the directory** check box. Then click **OK**.

14. To connect to your partner's printer, click the **Start** button and type **\\partner's_computer_name** in the *Search programs and files* box and press the **Enter** key.

15. Right-click the **partner's hplj5200 printer** and click **Connect**. It will take a minute or two to connect and automatically load the drivers from the computer.

16. Go back to the *Devices and Printers* dialog box.

Question 4	*Which printer is your partner's printer?*

Question 5	*You have confirmed that your partner's printer is installed, configured, and shared properly, yet a single computer running Windows 7 cannot connect to it or even browse to it. What is most likely the problem?*

17. From *Devices and Printers*, click the **HPLJ5200 on partner's_computer_name printer** and click **Manage default printers** from the toolbar.

18. With the *Change my default printer when I change network* option selected, select the **Contoso01** network and select the **HPLJ5200 on partner's computer _name** printer. Click the **Update** button.

19. Click **OK** to close the *Manage Default Printers* dialog box.

Exercise 8.3 Troubleshooting Printing

Overview	At the Contoso Corporation, you have a network printer that was working fine yesterday but today no one can print to it. Therefore, you will need to determine what the problem is with the printer.
Completion time	35 minutes

1. Windows 7 includes a Printer Troubleshooter that detects if the printer is offline, out of paper, out of toner, or has a paper jam; if the printer spooler is not running or has an error; or if a print job is preventing other print jobs to print. To start the Printer Troubleshooter, click **Start** and then click **Control Panel**.

2. Click **System and Security**, and click **Troubleshoot Common Computer Problems** under *Action Center*.

3. Under *Hardware and Sound*, click **Use A Printer**.

4. When the Printer Troubleshooter appears, click the **Next** button.

5. If your printer is not listed, you would choose the **My Printer is not listed** option. For now, click the **HPLJ5200 on partner's computer _name** printer and click the **Next** button.

6. Assuming that it found no problems, click the **Close** button. If you do have problems, you will have to look at the messages that are displayed. If the printer is out of paper, out of toner, or has a paper jam, you will have to go to the printer and manually fix the problem. Then you may need to restart the printer for the printer to clear the error. Other error messages may require you to start the printer spooler and/or delete current print jobs (discussed later in this lab).

7. Open the *Devices and Printers* folder.

8. Click **a printer** and click the **Print Server Properties** option.

9. Click the **Security** tab.

Question 6	*Which user account or group and permission allows your partner to print?*

10. Click the **Ports** tab.

Question 7	*What is the port name?*

11. Open a *Command prompt* and try to **ping 10.10.0.241**.

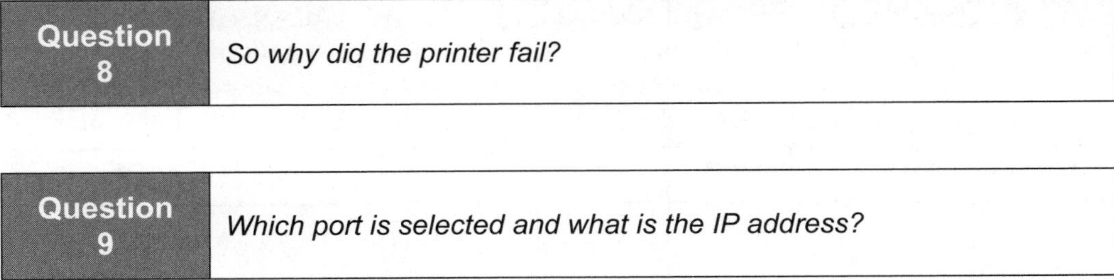

Question 8	*So why did the printer fail?*

Question 9	*Which port is selected and what is the IP address?*

12. Click the **Advanced** tab.

Question 10	*Where is the default spool folder?*

13. Click the **OK** button to close the *Print Server Properties* dialog box.

14. Right-click the **Network HPLJ5200** printer and select **Printer Properties**.

15. Click the **Ports** tab.

16. Verify the port by clicking the port assigned to the printer and clicking the **Configure Port** button. Then look at the IP address and port number—the default is 9100. By default, the name includes the IP address, but that can be modified.

17. Double-click the **HPLJ5200** printer.

18. Click the **See What's Printing** option. The print queue will show you which print jobs are queued and if the print jobs are progressing.

19. Take a screen shot of the printer's print queue by pressing **Alt+Prt Scr**, and then paste the resulting image into the Lab08_worksheet file in the page provided by pressing **Ctrl+V**.

20. Click the **Start** button, right-click **Computer**, and select **Manage**.

21. Click **Services** under the *Services and Applications* item.

22. Verify that the *Print Spooler* service is running (*Started* should be next to Print Spooler in the Status column). If it is not running, right-click the **Print Spooler** and select **Start**. If it fails to start, you will need to look at the error displayed and check the Windows System and Application logs in Event Viewer for error messages that you can research.

23. Right-click **Print Spooler** and select **Restart** to restart the service.

Question 11	*What other service besides the Print Spooler is required to run users to access shared resources including shared folders and printers?*

24. Verify that the *Server service* is running (*Started* should be next to Print Spooler in the Status column). If it is not running, right-click the **Print Spooler** and select **Start**. If it fails to start, you will need to look at the error displayed and check the Windows System and Application logs in Event Viewer.

25. Close the *Computer Management* console.

26. Click the **Start** button, click **All Programs**, and click **Accessories**. Then right-click **Command Prompt** and select **Run as Administrator**.

27. To stop the Print Spooler service using a command, execute the following command at the command prompt:

```
net stop spooler
```

28. To start the Print Spooler service, execute the following command at the command prompt:

```
net start spooler
```

29. If restarting the Print Spooler does not remove the current print jobs, you will first need to stop the Print Spooler service at the command prompt and delete any files in the spool file. Therefore, execute the **`net stop spooler`** command again.

30. Click the **Start** button, and click **Computer**. Then using Windows Explorer, navigate to the *C:\Windows\System32\Spool* folder. If there are any files in the Spool folder, delete them.

31. Use the **`net start spooler`** command to start the spooler again.

Question 12	*You just grabbed the newest printer driver from the Internet. However, when you print, it does not print the last two inches on the last page. What should you do?*

32. If the current print driver is having problems, you can try reinstalling the printer or use a different driver. To reinstall the printer driver, go back to Devices And Printers, right-click **HPLJ5200**, and click **Printer Properties**. Then select the *Advanced* tab and click **New Driver** to add a driver.

33. When the *Add Printer Driver Wizard* starts, click the **Next** button.

34. If you have downloaded a newer driver, you would click the **Have Disk…** button so that you can specify where the driver is. For now, if you have a connection to the Internet, click the **Windows Update** button. You will have to wait a few minutes while the driver list is updated.

35. Select **HP** for the *manufacturer* and **HP LaserJet 5200 Series PCL 5** for *Printers* and click the **Next** button. Note: If you performed the Windows Update, you may see a (HP) version and a (Microsoft version). If so, select the HP version.

36. When the wizard is complete, click the **Finish** button.

Question 13	*You are trying to print to a Windows shared printer. What would be a simple way to verify that you can see the shared printer for your partner's computer?*

Question 14	*What share permission will a user need to see the printer?*

37. To verify if the firewall will allow printing, click **Start** and click **Control Panel**.

38. Click **System and Security** and then click **Windows Firewall**. Note the current Network Location.

39. Click **Allow A Program Or Feature Through Windows Firewall**.

40. On the *Allowed Programs* window, make sure the *File And Printer Sharing* check box is selected. Click **OK**.

41. Log off of the computer.

LAB 9
DEALING WITH SOFTWARE ISSUES

This lab contains the following exercises and activities:

Exercise 9.1	Configuring Software Compatibility Options
Exercise 9.2	Installing Windows XP Mode
Exercise 9.3	Using the Standard User Analyzer
Exercise 9.4	Troubleshooting Windows Installer Issues

BEFORE YOU BEGIN

The lab environment consists of student workstations connected to a local area network, along with a server that functions as the domain controller for a domain called contoso.com. The computers required for this lab are listed in Table 9-1.

Table 9-1
Computers required for Lab 9

Computer	***Operating System***	***Computer Name***
Server	Windows Server 2008 R2	RWDC01
Workstation*xx* where *xx* is the student's number	Windows 7 Enterprise	NYC-CL*xx* where *xx* is the student's number

> **NOTE**
> *In a classroom lab environment, there will be one classroom server and the students will have workstations named using consecutive numbers in place of the xx and yy variables. In a virtual lab environment, each student will have three virtual machines, named RWDC01, NYC-CL1, and NYC-CL2.*

In addition to the computers, you will also require the software listed in Table 9-2 to complete Lab 9.

Table 9-2
Software required for Lab 9

Software	***Location***
Windows 7 XP Mode Files	\\rwdc01\dowloads\WindowsXPMode_en-us.exe \\rwdc01\dowloads\Windows6.1-KB977206-x64.exe \\rwdc01\dowloads\Windows6.1-KB958559-x64.exe
Lab 9 student worksheet	Lab09_worksheet.rtf (provided by instructor)

> **NOTE**
> *In this manual, we assume that the 64-bit version of Windows 7 is in use in the lab. If your lab uses the 32-bit version, you must use 32-bit versions for all additional software as well.*

Working with Lab Worksheets

Each lab in this manual requires that you answer questions, make screen shots, and perform other activities that you will document on a worksheet named for the lab, such as Lab09_worksheet.rtf. Your instructor will provide you with access to the worksheets. It is recommended that you use a USB flash drive to store your worksheets, so you can submit them to your instructor for review. As you perform the exercises in each lab, open the appropriate worksheet file using WordPad, fill in the required information, and save the file to your flash drive.

SCENARIO

You are working for the Contoso Corporation and have been assigned to test applications running under Windows 7. Therefore, your task is to test various applications and to figure out the best way to get several older applications to run under Windows 7.

After completing this lab, you will be able to:

- Configure an older application to work with Windows 7
- Mitigate applications that do not run well under User Access Control
- Troubleshoot installing msi programs under Windows 7

Estimated lab time: 75 minutes

Exercise 9.1	Configuring Software Compatibility Options
Overview	You have a several programs that were written for Windows XP. When you install these programs on new computers running Windows 7, the applications will not run. Therefore, during this exercise, you will look at various options in troubleshooting the installation and running of older programs.
Completion time	15 minutes

1. Turn on the NYC-CL*xx* workstation and log on using the **contoso\Administrator** account and the password **Pa$$w0rd**.

2. Open the *\\rwdc01\download* folder using the *Search program and files* text box and open the *flmath95* folder.

3. Double-click the **setup.exe** file and click **OK** to install followed by clicking the **Computer** button. Click the **Install Now** button. If you are presented with a message indicating that you do not have enough disk space, continue by clicking the **Install Now** button.

Question 1	*What error message did you get?*

4. Click **Abort** and then click the **Yes** button to quit the product setup. Click the **OK** button.

5. Click **OK** a second time to start the application removal utility to remove temporary installation files.

6. Click the **Remove All** button to remove shared components. Click the **OK** button. When the program has been removed, click the **OK** button.

7. When it asks to delete the installation log file, click the **Yes** button.

8. Right-click the **Setup.exe** and select Properties.

9. Click the *Compatibility* tab.

Question 2	*What is the default operating system for Windows 7 Compatibility mode?*

Question 3	*If the program will not run under a standard user account, what option should you select?*

10. Select the **Run this program in compatibility mode** option. Since this program was made for Windows 95, select **Windows 95**. Click **OK**.

11. Try to reinstall the *flmath95* program again. The same error occurs.

12. Right-click **setup.exe**. Make sure *compatibility mode* is selected and select the **Run this program as an administrator** option. Click the **OK** button.

13. Try to reinstall the *flmath95* program once more. Although you are running the program in Windows 95 compatibility mode and you are running the program as an administrator, the same error occurs.

14. Right-click the **Setup.exe** program once more and select **Troubleshoot compatibility**.

15. Click the **Try recommended settings** option.

Question 4	*What compatibility mode is the troubleshooter recommended?*

16. Click to **Start** the program.

17. Try to install the program again. You might again receive a message indicating you do not have enough disk space. Ignore the message and continue with the installation.

18. When the program is successfully installed, click the **OK** button.

19. Back at the *Program Compatibility* page, click the **Next** button.

20. Click **Yes**, save these settings for this program.

21. Click the **Close** button.

Exercise 9.2	Installing Windows XP Mode
Overview	When you cannot run an application using the program compatibility options or troubleshooter, you can try to use Windows XP Mode to run the older application. During this exercise, you will install and configure Windows XP Mode and install an application written for Windows 95.
Completion time	25 minutes

1. Open and run **\\rwdc01\dowloads\WindowsXPMode_en-us.exe** using the *Search Programs and Files* text box. If it asks if you want to run this file, click the **Run** button.

2. When the welcome screen appears, click the **Next** button.

3. When it asks for the location, click the **Next** button.

4. When the setup is complete, click the **Finish** button.

5. Open and run **\\rwdc01\dowloads\Windows6.1-KB958559-x64.exe** using the *Search Programs and Files* text box. When it asks if you want to install the application, click the **Yes** button.

6. When the license agreement appears, click the **I Accept** button.

7. When it asks to restart the computer, click the **Restart Now** button.

8. Log in to the Windows 7 computer and execute **\\rwdc01\dowloads\Windows6.1-KB977206-x64.exe** using the *Search Programs and Files* text box When it asks if you want to install this update, click the **Yes** button.

9. When it asks to restart the computer, click **Restart Now**.

10. Log in to the Windows 7 computer.

11. Click the **Start** button, select **All Programs**, select **Windows Virtual PC** and select **Windows XP Mode**.

12. When the *Windows XP Mode License* appears, click the **I accept the license terms** option and click the **Next** button.

13. When it asks for the *password*, type **Pa$$w0rd** and click the **Next** button.

14. When it asks to help protect your computer, click the **Not right now** option and click the **Next** button.

15. Click the **Start Setup** button. When the setup is done, you should have a virtual XP environment running on your computer running Windows 7.

16. Click the **Start** button, click **Windows Virtual PC** and select **Windows XP Mode**.

17. Click the **Start** button in the *Windows XP Mode* window, right-click **My Computer** and select **Properties**.

Question 5	*What edition, version, and service pack of Windows XP is running?*

18. Click **OK** to close the *System Properties* dialog box.

19. Click the **Start** button and click **My Computer**.

Question 6	*How would you access the C drive on the Windows 7 machine?*

20. Double-click the **C drive** on the Windows 7 machine within the *Windows XP Mode* window.

21. Close the **C drive** on the Windows 7 machine.

22. Click the Windows XP **Start** button and select the **Run** option. Type **\\rwdc01\download** and click the **OK** button.

23. Open the *flmath95* folder, double-click **setup.exe**, and install the flmath95 program.

Question 7	*Did you have any problems installing the program?*

24. Open the *Windows XP Mode Action* menu and click the **Close** button.

Exercise 9.3	Using the Standard User Analyzer
Overview	Sometimes applications running under Windows 7 do not run well under User Account Control (UAC). These applications can be configured to run properly with UAC by using the Standard User Analyzer that is included with Application Compatibility Toolkit (ACT). During this exercise, you will test and modify the Stock Viewer demo application to run under Windows 7 and UAC.
Completion time	15 minutes

1. Open *Internet Explorer* and go to the Microsoft website. Search for and download *Microsoft Application Verifier* to your Desktop.

2. Double-click the **ApplicationVerifier** executable file. When the wizard starts, click the **Next** button.

3. When it displays the *End-User License Agreement*, click the **I accept the terms in the License Agreement** option and click the **Next** button.

4. When it is ready to install, click the **Install** button. If it asks if the program is allowed to be installed, click the **Yes** button.

5. When the program is installed, click the **Finish** button.

6. Using the Microsoft website, search for *Microsoft Application Compatibility Toolkit (ApplicationCompatibilityToolkitSetup.exe)*. Then download the newest version of ACT to your desktop.

7. Double-click the **ApplicationCompatibilityToolkitSetup.exe** on the desktop. If it asks if you will allow ACT to make changes to your computer, click the **Yes** button.

8. When the *ACT Setup wizard* opens, click the **Next** button.

9. Select the **I accept the terms in the License Agreement** option and click the **Next** button.

10. When it asks for the *Destination* folder, click the **Next** button.

11. When it is ready to install ACT, click the **Install** button.

12. When ACT is installed, click the **Finish** button.

13. Click the **Start** button, select **All Programs**, select **Microsoft Application Compatibility Toolkit**, select **Developer and Tester Tools**, and then click **Standard User Analyzer Wizard**.

14. In the *Standard User Analyzer* window, click the **Browse For Application** button. Then navigate to *C:\Program Files\Microsoft Application Compatibility Toolkit\Compatibility Administrator (32-bit)\Demo Application\StockViewer* folder and click **StockViewer**, Then click **Open**.

15. Click the **Launch** button.

16. If it warns you to delete all AppVerifier logs, click the **Yes** button. If it asks you to continue, click the **Yes** button.

17. In the *Permission denied* window, click the **OK** button.

18. In *Stock Viewer*, click the **Trends** button. When it says that it is unable to show trends, click the **OK** button.

19. In *Stock Viewer*, open the **Tools** menu, and select **Options**.

20. When the unhandled exception has occurred, click the **Details** button. Then after reviewing the messages, click the **Continue** button.

21. Close Stock Viewer.

22. In *Standard User Analyzer Wizard*, it asks if the application finished without any problems. Click the **No** button. The Standard User Analyzer Wizard displays the potential mitigations for the application.

23. Click the **Launch** button. It may take a minute or so for Stock Viewer to open.

24. In *Stock Viewer*, click the **Trends** button.

25. In *Stock Viewer*, open the **Tools** menu, and then click **Options**.

26. When Stock Viewer opens a *No Options Available* dialog box appears, click the **OK** button.

27. Close Stock Viewer.

28. When *Standard User Analyzer Wizard* asks if the application finish running without any problems, click the **Yes** button.

29. Click the **Export** button to export the mitigations for the Stock Viewer application to an MSI file, which can be distributed to your clients. Save the msi file to your desktop.

30. When the msi file has been saved, click the **OK** button.

31. Click the **Exit** button to close the Standard User Analyzer Wizard.

32. Double-click the **msi file** that you just created to apply changes to your system so that it can make the necessary adjustments for Stock Viewer to run on a system running Windows 7 with UAC enabled. When it asks you to allow the program from an unknown publisher, you would need to determine if this application is safe to run. Since it was an application that you just created, click the **Yes** button.

33. Click the **Start** button, click **Microsoft Application Compatibility Toolkit**, click **Demo Application**, and click **Stock Viewer**.

34. Test the application by clicking the **Trends** button.

35. Close Stock Viewer.

Exercise 9.4	Troubleshooting Windows Installer Issues
Overview	If you have problems installing a .msi program including when you receive a "MSIEXEC.exe has encountered problem" error message, it usually indicates that there is a problem with the Windows Installer. During this exercise, you will look at ways to troubleshoot the Windows installer.
Completion time	20 minutes

1. If you are having problems installing a program, you should first try to reboot the computer to make sure that another program installation is not interfering with the installation. Next, you should verify that Windows Installer is functioning by clicking the **Start** button, executing the **`msiexec`** command using the *Search programs and files* text box, and pressing the **Enter** key.

2. When the *Windows Installer* dialog box appears, click the **OK** button.

3. If the Windows Installer dialog box did not appear, you need to make sure that the Windows installer service is not disabled. Therefore, you need to first click the **Start** button, right-click **Computer**, and select **Manage**. Then expand *Services and Application* and click **Services**.

4. Find the Windows installer and verify that startup type is either Automatic or manual. If the Windows installer is disabled, right-click **Windows Installer** and select **Properties**. Then change the *Startup type* to **Automatic** and click the **OK** button.

5. Next, you should verify that the Windows Installer status is started. If Windows Installer is not started, you should verify that it the Windows Installer can start by right-clicking **Windows Installer** and selecting **Start**.

6. If Windows Installer does not start, you should try to reregister the Windows installer at the command prompt. Click the **Start** button, select **All Programs**, select **Accessories**, right-click **Command Prompt**, and select **Run as administrator**.

7. To reregister the Windows Installer, execute the following commands at the command prompt:

   ```
   Msiexec /unregister

   Msiexec /register
   ```

8. If the msiexec still does not run, you should search for and download the latest version of Windows Installer. Of course, before you look for the newest version, you should first look to see which version of msiexec you have. Click the **Start** button and click **Computer**. Then double-click the **C drive**, double-click the **Windows** folder, and double-click the **System32** folder.

9. Right-click the **msiexec.exe** file and select **Properties**. Then click the **Details** tab.

Question 8	*What version of the Windows Installer do you have?*

10. Click **OK** to close the *Properties* dialog box.

11. To run Windows updates, click the **Start** button, select **All Programs**, and select **Windows Updates**.

12. Click the **Check for updates** button. If it asks you to install new Windows Update software, click the **Install Now** button. Then rerun the Windows Updates again.

13. Windows Update will take a couple of minutes to retrieve a list of available updates. When Windows is done searching, click the **XX important updates are available** option. Review the available updates and select any updates that you see as important that are not already selected including Windows 7 Service Pack 1 (or higher). Then click the **OK** button.

14. Click the **Install updates** button.

15. After the updates have been installed, click the **Restart Now** button, and reboot the computer.

LAB 10
MANAGING AND MONITORING PERFORMANCE

This lab contains the following exercises and activities:

Exercise 10.1	Analyzing Performance
Exercise 10.2	Configuring Virtual Memory
Exercise 10.3	Configuring Power Options

BEFORE YOU BEGIN

The lab environment consists of student workstations connected to a local area network, along with a server that functions as the domain controller for a domain called contoso.com. The computers required for this lab are listed in Table 10-1.

Table 10-1
Computers required for Lab 10

Computer	*Operating System*	*Computer Name*
Server	Windows Server 2008 R2	RWDC01
Workstation*xx* where *xx* is the student's number	Windows 7 Enterprise	NYC-CL*xx* where *xx* is the student's number

> **NOTE**
> *In a classroom lab environment, there will be one classroom server and the students will have workstations named using consecutive numbers in place of the* xx *and* yy *variables. In a virtual lab environment, each student will have three virtual machines, named RWDC01, NYC-CL1, and NYC-CL2.*

In addition to the computers, you will also require the software listed in Table 10-2 to complete Lab 10.

Table 10-2
Software required for Lab 10

Software	***Location***
MemAlloc Program	\\rwdc01\dowloads\MemAlloc.exe
Lab 10 student worksheet	Lab10_worksheet.rtf (provided by instructor)

Working with Lab Worksheets

Each lab in this manual requires that you answer questions, make screen shots, and perform other activities that you will document on a worksheet named for the lab, such as Lab10_worksheet.rtf. Your instructor will provide you with access to the worksheets. It is recommended that you use a USB flash drive to store your worksheets, so you can submit them to your instructor for review. As you perform the exercises in each lab, open the appropriate worksheet file using WordPad, fill in the required information, and save the file to your flash drive.

SCENARIO

You are a newly hired desktop technician for Contoso Ltd. and have been assigned to work on a long-term test deployment of some new Windows 7 workstations. Your job is to track the computers' performance levels over the course of a week and determine which components, if any, are negatively affecting system performance.

After completing this lab, you will be able to:

- Monitor system performance using the Performance Monitor console
- Change the paging file settings to improve performance
- Configure power settings to balance performance and battery life

Estimated lab time: 50 minutes

Exercise 10.1 Analyzing Performance

Overview	You just logged in to your computer at Contoso Ltd. And you notice that your computer seems to be running extremely slow. You suspect that some program is utilizing too many resources. Therefore, you decide to look at Task Manager, Resource Manager, and Performance Monitor to give you a glimpse of the system's performance.
Completion time	25 minutes

1. Turn on the NYC-CL*xx* workstation and log on using the **contoso\Administrator** account and the password **Pa$$w0rd**.
2. Right-click the task bar and click **Start Task Manager**.
3. Click **Applications** for current applications that are running.
4. Click the **New Task** button. Type **Wordpad** and press the **Enter** key. Notice that WordPad opens and is now listed in the Applications tab.
5. Click the **Processes** tab.
6. Click the **CPU** header at the top of the window to sort by *CPU utilization*.
7. Click the **Image Name** header at the top of the window to sort by *process names*.
8. Find and right-click the **Wordpad** process. Then select **End Process**. When it asks if you want to end wordpad.exe, click the **End** process button.
9. Click the **Services** tab to list all of the services running.
10. Click the **Performance** tab.
11. Using the *Start* button and *Search programs and files* text box, open the **\\rwdc01\downloads** folder and copy **MemAlloc.exe** to your desktop.
12. Double-click the **MemAlloc.exe**.
13. Click **Allocate memory** every couple of seconds until you get the *Out of Memory* error message. Notice the physical memory Usage History and the amount of Physical Memory used.
14. In *Task Manager*, click the **Processes** tab.
15. To sort by memory used, click the **Memory (Private Working Set)** header so that the amount of memory that an applications uses most is at the top of the list.
16. Click the **Performance** tab.

17. Click the **Resource Monitor** button.

18. Click the **small up arrow (^)** to expand Memory. Notice the PID and memory usage of the MemAlloc.exe.

19. In *Resource Monitor*, click the **Memory** tab. The Memory tab will show you how much physical memory is in use and how much is free. It also shows you several graphs including Used Physical Memory, Commit Charge, and hard Faults/sec.

Question 1	*What is indicated when there is a Hard Faults/sec while having high Physical Memory use?*

20. Close Resource Monitor.

21. Close the MemAlloc.exe program. Notice that the Physical Memory Usage drops.

22. Close Task Manager.

23. Open the **Control Panel**. Click **System And Security > Administrative Tools**. Then click **Performance Monitor**. The Performance Monitor console appears.

24. Expand *Data Collector Sets*, expand *System*, and then click **System Diagnostics**.

25. Right-click **System Diagnostics** and click **Start**. Wait a minute for the System Diagnostic to stop running.

26. Right-click the **System Performance** and click **Start**. Wait 60 seconds for each test to complete in order for the System Performance to stop running.

27. Right-click **System Diagnostics** and select **Latest Report**.

28. When the report is displayed, browse through the report to see what is in it.

29. Right-click **System Performance** and select **Latest Report**.

30. When the report is displayed, browse through the report to see what is in it.

31. Expand *Monitoring Tools* and select **Performance Monitor**.

32. Click the **View Log Data** button on the toolbar to open the *Performance Monitor Properties* dialog box and select **Log Files**. Click **Add** and select the *C:\Perflogs\System\Diagnostics\<Computer_Name>_yyyymmdd-######\Performance Counter.blg* file to open the performance counter log created when you ran the System Diagnostics data collector set. Click **Open**. Click **OK** to return to Performance Monitor.

33. Click the **Add** button (the button with the green plus sign) on the toolbar to add the following counters to the chart and then click **OK**:

    - *Processor\% Processor Time*
    - *Memory\% Committed Bytes In Use*
    - *PhysicalDisk\Disk Bytes/sec*
    - *System\Processes*
    - *System\Processor Queue Length*

34. If you have trouble seeing some of the counters—especially if the line being graphed is at the bottom or top of the graph—click the counter and press **Ctrl+H**.

35. Click the **Change Graph Type** button and select **Histogram bar**.

36. Click the **Change Graph Type** button and select **Report**.

37. Close the Computer Management console.

Exercise 10.2	Configuring Virtual Memory
Overview	Virtual memory includes disk space that is used as memory. In Windows, the paging file is virtual memory. To get the best performance, you must make sure you have enough RAM and that you configure the paging file. In this exercise, you will look at changing the paging file options.
Completion time	10 minutes

1. Click the **Start** button, right-click **Computer** and select **Computer Management**.

2. In *Computer Management*, expand *Storage* and click **Disk Management**.

3. Using Disk Management, right-click the **free disk space** and select **New Simple Volume**.

4. When the *New Simple Volume Wizard* opens, click the **Next** button.

5. Enter **20000** for the *Simple volume in size in MB* and click the **Next** button.

6. Assign the *E* drive and click the **Next** button.

7. For the *Volume Label*, type **Paging** and click the **Next** button.

8. Close Computer Management.

9. Click the **Start** button, Right-click **Computer** and select **Properties**.

10. Click **Advanced System Settings**.

11. Click the **Advanced** tab.

12. Click the **Settings** button in the *Performance* section.

13. Click the **Advanced** tab in the *Performance Options*.

14. In the *Virtual Memory*, click the **Change** button.

15. Deselect the *Automatically manage paging file size for all drives* section.

16. Select **E:** and click the **Custom size** option. Specify **2048** for the *Initial size (MB) and Maximum size (MB)*. Click the **Set** button.

17. Select **C:** and select the **No paging file** option. Click the **Set** button.

18. Click **OK** to close the *Virtual Memory* dialog box.

19. Click **OK** to close the *System Properties* dialog box.

20. When it asks you to reboot Windows, click the **Restart Now** button.

Exercise 10.3 Configuring Power Options

Overview	When using mobile computers, you usually want the best performance with the best battery life. Therefore, during this exercise you will configure various power settings including hibernation settings and power schemes.
Completion time	15 minutes

1. Click the **Start** button and click **Computer**. Double-click the **C drive**.

2. Press and release the **Alt** key, then click the **Tools** menu and select the **Folder options** option.

3. Click the **View** tab.

4. Select the **Show hidden files, folders, or drives** option and deselect the *Hide protected operating System files (Recommended)* option. When it asks if you are sure you want to display these files, click the **Yes** button. Click **OK** to close the Folder Options.

Question 2	*How large is the pagefile?*

Question 3	*Do you have a hibernat.fil file? If you do, how big is the file?*

5. If you do not have the hibernat.fil file, execute the following command at an elevated command prompt:

   `Powercfg -h on`

   Notice the size of the hiberfil.sys file.

6. To disable hibernate, execute the following command:

   `Powercfg -h off`

   Notice that the hiberfil.sys file disappears.

7. Use the **`powercfg`** command to enable the hibernate feature.

8. Close the command prompt.

9. Click the **Start** button and select **Control Panel**. Then select **System and Security** and select **Power Options**.

10. Click the **Change when the computer sleeps** option.

Question 4	*When does the computer sleep?*

11. Click the **Change Advanced power settings** option.

12. Expand *Sleep*.

13. Expand the *Hibernate after* option.

Question 5	*So when does the system hibernate?*

14. Click **OK** to close Power Options.

15. Click **Cancel** to close the Edit Plan Settings.

16. Make sure *Balanced [Active]* is selected. Then click the **Change plan settings** option next in the *Balanced (recommended option)* section.

17. Click the **Cancel** button to close the *Edit Plan Settings* dialog box.

Question 6	*If you are back on the Power options window, which option would you chose of you want to disable a laptop from sleeping or hibernating when you close the lid?*

18. Click the **Choose what the power button does** option. Look at the different options available. If you have a desktop, you most likely will have only the *When I press the power button* option. If you have a mobile computer, you most likely will also have the *When I press the sleep button* option and the *When I close the lid* option.

19. Click the **Cancel** button.

Question 7	*On a laptop computer, which component most likely consumes the most power?*

20. At the bottom of the *Power Options* screen, adjust the brightness halfway and look at how the screen adjusts.

21. Readjust the screen brightness to your preference.

22. Close the Control Panel.

LAB 11
CONFIGURING AND TROUBLESHOOTING INTERNET EXPLORER

This lab contains the following exercises and activities:

Exercise 11.1	Configuring and Testing Internet Explorer
Exercise 11.2	Troubleshooting Internet Explorer
Exercise 11.3	Using Group Policies with Internet Explorer

BEFORE YOU BEGIN

The lab environment consists of student workstations connected to a local area network, along with a server that functions as the domain controller for a domain called contoso.com. The computers required for this lab are listed in Table 11-1.

Table 11-1
Computers required for Lab 11

Computer	*Operating System*	*Computer Name*
Server	Windows Server 2008 R2	RWDC01
Workstation*xx* where *xx* is the student's number	Windows 7 Enterprise	NYC-CL*xx* where *xx* is your student number

NOTE

In a classroom lab environment, there will be one classroom server and the students will have workstations named using consecutive numbers in place of the xx *and* yy *variables. In a virtual lab environment, each student will have three virtual machines, named RWDC01, NYC-CL01, and NYC-CL02.*

In addition to the computers, you will also require the software listed in Table 11-2 to complete Lab 11.

Table 11-2
Software required for Lab 11

Software	***Location***
Lab 11 student worksheet	Lab11_worksheet.rtf (provided by instructor)

NOTE

We assume you are using the 64-bit version of Windows 7 in your lab. If you are using the 32-bit version of Windows 7, you must use 32-bit versions of other software as well.

Working with Lab Worksheets

Each lab in this manual requires that you answer questions, make screen shots, and perform other activities that you will document on a worksheet named for the lab, such as Lab11_worksheet.rtf. Your instructor will provide you with access to the worksheets. It is recommended that you use a USB flash drive to store your worksheets, so you can submit them to your instructor for review. As you perform the exercises in each lab, open the appropriate worksheet file using WordPad, fill in the required information, and save the file to your flash drive.

SCENARIO

You are a Windows 7 technical specialist for Contoso Ltd. a company with workstations in a variety of different environments. As part of your company's ongoing evaluation of Windows 7, you have been asked to explore the best configuration of Internet Explorer for your company while troubleshooting a couple of reported problems.

After completing this lab, you will be able to:

- Configure Internet Explorer
- Troubleshoot Internet Explorer
- Lock down Internet Explorer

Estimated lab time: 50 minutes

Exercise 11.1	Configuring and Testing Internet Explorer
Overview	The director of IT at Contoso Ltd. wants you to reconfigure and test Internet Explorer on various computers so that it will run better with certain applications.
Completion time	30 minutes

1. Turn on the NYC-CL*xx* workstation and log on using the **contoso\Administrator** account and the password **Pa$$w0rd**.
2. Start Internet Explorer and open **http://www.microsoft.com**.
3. Click the **Tools** button and select **Internet Options**.
4. To make www.microsoft.com your home page, click the **Use current button** in the *Home page* section.
5. To clear your history, click the **Delete** button in the *Browsing history* section.
6. With the default options already specified, click the **Delete** button.
7. Click the **Security** tab.

Question 1	*At the bottom of the Internet Explorer window, what zone is the www.microsoft.com website?*

8. Click **Trusted sites**.
9. To add www.microsoft.com to the trusted site list, click the **Sites** button. http://www.microsoft.com should already be in the *Add this website to this zone* text box. Deselect the *Require server verification (https:) for all sites in this zone* option. Click the **Add** button. Click the **Close** button.
10. Press the **F5** key on the keyboard.

Question 2	*At the bottom of the Internet Explorer window, what zone does www.microsoft.com website show now?*

11. The zone is mixed because www.microsoft .com contains other components including update.microsoft.com. Therefore, part of it is considered in the Trusted zone, while other parts of the page are considered in the Internet zone. Click the **Tools** button and select **Internet Options**.
12. Click the **Security** tab and select **Trusted sites**. Click the **Sites** button.

13. Click **www.microsoft.com** and click the **Remove** button.

14. In the *Add this website to the zone* text box, type ***.microsoft.com**. Click the **Add** button.

15. Click the **Close** button to close the *Trusted sites* dialog box.

16. Click **OK** to close the *Internet Options* dialog box.

17. Press the **F5** key on the keyboard. Notice that the webpage is still Unknown zone because there are other components that do not follow the *.microsoft.com.

18. Click the **Tools** button and select **Internet Options**.

19. Click the **Security** tab and click the **Internet zone**.

20. Click the **Custom level** button.

Question 3	*If you click the Reset custom settings option, what level is the default?*

Question 4	*Under ActiveX controls and plug-ins what option is selected for Allow previously unused ActiveX controls to run without prompt?*

21. Click the **Cancel** button to close the security settings for the Internet zone.

22. Click the **Privacy** tab.

23. To make sure a particular site does not have pop-up windows blocked, click the **Settings** button under the *Pop-up Blocker*.

24. Type **www.microsoft.com** in the *Address of Website to allow* area and click the **Add** button.

25. Click the **Close** button to close the *Pop-up blocking Settings* dialog box.

26. Click the **Connections** tab.

27. Click the **LAN settings** button under the *Local Area Network (LAN) settings* section.

28. If the *Automatically detect settings* option is selected, deselect the option.

29. To show how you would use a proxy server to connect to the Internet, assuming your organization has one, select the **Use a proxy server for your LAN**. A proxy server allows multiple users to share one or more public addresses so that they can access the Internet at the same time. It also provides security for the internal users while giving an organization control of the user's Internet connection. To determine if your organization is using a proxy server, you would have to contact your network administrator for the organization's network. If you have set IP configuration properly to connect to the network and still cannot connect to the Internet, there is a good chance the organization is using a proxy server.

30. Type **172.24.255.20** for the address and specify port **8080**. Also select the **Bypass proxy server for local addresses** option. Common ports used for proxy servers are 8080 and 3127.

31. Click **OK** to close the *Local Area Network (LAN) Settings* dialog box and click the **OK** button to close the *Internet Options* dialog box.

32. Try to access the Microsoft website using Internet Explorer. Since there really isn't a proxy server on our network, you need to reset the settings back to automatic.

33. Go back into the *Local Area Network (LAN) Settings* again and deselect the *Use a proxy server for your LAN*. Select the **Automatically detect settings** option.

34. Click **OK** to close the *Local Area Network (LAN) Settings* dialog box and click the **OK** button to close the *Internet Options* dialog box.

35. Try to access the Microsoft website to make sure that you are connected to the Internet again.

36. Click the **Tools** button and select **Internet Options**.

37. Click the **Programs** tab.

38. Click the **Manage add-ons** button.

39. Review the Toolbars and Extensions, Search Providers, Accelerators, and InPrivate Filtering to see your managed add-ons.

40. Close the *Manage Add-ons* dialog box.

41. Go to the *www.adobe.com* and install the Adobe reader. If you don't have Internet access, go to *\\rwdc01\downloads* to access the Adobe Reader.

42. In Internet Explorer, click **Tools** and select **Manage Add-ons**.

Question 5	*What new Add-in was added to Internet Explorer?*

43. Close the *Manage Add-ons* window.

44. Open the *http://www.ieaddons.com* website with Internet Explorer.

45. Click **Get Add-ons**.

46. Find and click **Wikipedia Visual Search**. Click the **Click to install** option. When it asks if you want to add this search provider, click the **Add** button.

47. Open the **Tools** menu and select **Manage Add-ons**.

48. Click **Search Providers** and verify that you have Wikipedia search provider.

49. Click **Wikipedia** and click the **Remove** button.

50. Click the **Close** button to close *Manage Add-ons*.

51. Click the **Start** button and then click **All Programs**. Then right-click **Internet Explorer** and click **Run as Administrator**.

52. Open the *http://www.microsoft.com* website.

53. Now open the *https://www.microsoft.com* website. Note that you are opening secure http (https). If it asks you if you want to view only the webpage that was delivered securely, click the **Yes** button.

54. Click the **lock at the top of the screen** and click the **View certificates** option.

55. Click the **Details** tab.

56. View the details of the Microsoft's digital certificate.

Question 6	*What signature algorithm does the certificate use?*

57. Click the **Certification Path** tab.

Question 7	*What name appears at the top of the Certification Path?*

58. Go back to the **General** tab.

59. Click the **Install Certificate** button.

60. When the *Welcome to the Certificate Import Wizard* appears, click the **Next** button.

61. Select the **Automatically select the certificate store based on the type of certificate** and click the **Next** button.

62. Click the **Finish** button.

63. When the import is successful, click **OK**.

64. Click **OK** to close the *Certificate* dialog box.

65. Click the **Start** button and enter **mmc** in the *Search programs and files* text box.

66. Click the **File** option and select the **Add/Remove Snap-in**.

67. Select **Certificates** and click the **Add** button.

68. Select **My User account** and click the **Next** button.

69. With *Local computer* selected, click the **Finish** button.

70. Click the **OK** button to close the *Add or Remove snap-ins* dialog box.

71. Expand *Certificates* > *Personal* and click the **Certificates** folder.

72. Double-click the **www.microsoft.com** certificate and notice it is the same certificate that you were viewing before.

73. Close the certificate.

74. Close the MMC console. If it asks you to save the console, click **No**.

75. Go back to Internet Explorer and access **http://www.hp.com**. The HP website opens successfully although it may change the actual URL.

76. Try to access **https://www.hp.com**.

Question 8	*You are asked: Do you want to view only the webpage content that was delivered securely? So what is the problem?*

77. To see http and https components, click the **No** button.

78. Try to access **https:/hp.com**.

Question 9	*What error message did you get?*

When you get this type of error message, you must determine if it is safe to continue. While it is not obvious by looking at the screen, this problem has occurred because the digital certificate is for www.hp.com and you are accessing hp.com.

Since the Hewlett-Packard website is most likely not going to be a security threat, you decide that it will be safe to continue. Therefore, click the **Continue to this website (not recommended)** link.

79. Close Internet Explorer.

Exercise 11.2	Troubleshooting Internet Explorer
Overview	The director of IT at Contoso Ltd. wants to prevent the company's Windows 7 users from modifying the default Internet Explorer configuration by installing additional software, such as add-ons and accelerators. Unfortunately, some clients are having problems visiting certain websites and you are assigned to investigate these problems.
Completion time	10 minutes

1. Start Internet Explorer.

2. Click the **Tools** option and select **Compatibility View Settings**. If you have a website that is not compatible with Internet Explorer, you would type the URL in the *Add this website* box and click the **Add** button.

3. Click the **Close** button.

4. Click the **Tools** menu and select **Internet Options**.

5. Click the **Advanced** tab.

6. Deselect *Show friendly HTTP* error messages option under the *Browsing* section. Sometimes when you get an error message, it may benefit you to deselect this option so that you get a more meaningful error message.

7. Under security, enable the following settings:

    - *Allow active content from CDs to run on My Computer*
    - *Allow active content to run in files on My Computer*

    These options may be needed when you need to run active content (such as JavaScript, Java applets, and ActiveX controls) from a CD or a network share.

8. Under *Browsing*, notice the *Enable third-party browser extensions* option. This option is usually used as a troubleshooting option that, when deselected, will disable third-party browser extensions that include search features, pop-up blockers, form auto-fill, and other features. Some common third-party browser extensions include Google Toolbar, Yahoo Toolbar, and Windows Live Toolbar.

9. Browse through the other options under the *Advanced* settings.

10. Click the **Reset** button. If you or an application made changes to Internet Explorer and you discover that Internet Explorer is unstable, you should try *Restore advanced settings* or click the **Reset** button.

11. Click the **Reset** button when it asks if you want to reset all Internet Explorer settings. When it warns you that you have to restart Internet Explorer, click **OK**.

12. Click the **Tools** option and click the **Manage Add-ons** option. Often Add-ons can cause problems with Internet Explorer.

13. To disable the Adobe PDF Link Helper, click the **Adobe PDF Link Helper** and click the **Disable** button. Note: if the add-in is already disabled, first click **Enable**.

14. To re-enable the Adobe PDF Link Helper, click the **Enable** button.

15. Close all Internet Explorer windows.

Exercise 11.3	Using Group Policies with Internet Explorer
Overview	The director of IT at Contoso Ltd. wants to prevent the company's Windows 7 users from modifying certain default Internet Explorer configurations by installing additional software, such as add-ons and accelerators. Therefore, you have been assigned to look at how to lock down Internet Explorer.
Completion time	10 minutes

1. Click the **Start** button, type **mmc** in the *Search programs and files* text box and press the **Enter** key. If Windows asks if you are sure you want to make changes to your system, click the **Yes** button.

2. Open the **File** menu and click **Add/Remove Snap in**.

3. Double-click **Group Policy Object Editor**. When *Welcome to the Group Policy Wizard* appears, click the **Finish** button so that you can look at local group policies.

4. Click the **OK** button to close the *Add or Remove snap-ins* option.

5. Maximize the MMC windows by clicking the **Maximize** button.

6. Expand *Local Computer Policy*, expand *Computer Configuration*, expand *Administrative Templates*, expand *Windows Components,* and expand *Internet Explorer*.

7. Click **Internet Explorer** within the MMC.

8. Browse through all the settings that are available for group policies.

9. To prevent users from enabling or disabling add-ons, double-click **Do not allow users to enable or disable add-ons**.

10. When the *Do not allow users to enable or disable add-ons* dialog box appears, read the Help box. Then click **Enable** and click the **OK** button.

11. Start Internet Explorer.

12. Open the **Tools** menu and select **Manage Add-ons**.

13. Click the **Adobe PDF Link Helper** and notice that the *Disable* button is grayed out.

14. Click the **Close** button to close the Manage Add-ons window.

15. Close Internet Explorer.

16. Go back to MMC and double-click **Do not allow users to enable or disable add-ons**.

17. Click the **Not Configured** option and click the **OK** button.

18. Start Internet Explorer.

19. Open the **Tools** menu and select **Manage Add-ons**.

20. Click the **Adobe PDF Link Helper** and notice that the *Disable* button is still grayed out. Sometimes when group policies are enabled, they must be disabled to undo the change.

21. Click the **Close** button to close the Manage Add-ons window.

22. Close Internet Explorer.

23. Go back to MMC and double-click **Do not allow users to enable or disable add-ons**.

24. Click the **Disabled** option and click the **OK** button.

25. Start Internet Explorer.

26. Open the **Tools** menu and select **Manage Add-ons**.

27. Click the **Adobe PDF Link Helper** and notice that the *Disable* button is no longer grayed out.

28. Click the **Close** button to close the Manage Add-ons window.

29. Close Internet Explorer.

30. On the MMC, expand the *Internet Control Panel* folder.

31. Double-click **Disable the Advanced page**.

32. Double-click **Enabled** and click the **OK** button.

33. Start Internet Explorer.

34. Open the **Tools** menu and select **Internet Options**. Notice the *Advanced* tab is no longer present.

35. Go back to the MMC and double-click the **Disable the Advanced page**.

36. Click the **Disabled** option and click the **OK** button.

37. Start Internet Explorer.

38. Open the **Tools** menu and select **Internet Options**. The *Advanced* tab is available again.

LAB 12
RESOLVING SECURITY SETTINGS

This lab contains the following exercises and activities:

Exercise 12.1 Configuring Windows Firewall

Exercise 12.2 Using Windows Defender

Exercise 12.3 Looking at Encrypting File System

Exercise 12.4 Using BitLocker

BEFORE YOU BEGIN

The lab environment consists of student workstations connected to a local area network, along with a server that functions as the domain controller for a domain called contoso.com. The computers required for this lab are listed in Table 12-1.

Table 12-1
Computers required for Lab 12

Computer	*Operating System*	*Computer Name*
Server	Windows Server 2008 R2	RWDC01
Workstation*xx* where *xx* is the student's number	Windows 7 Enterprise	NYC-CL*xx* where *xx* is your student number

> **NOTE**
> *In a classroom lab environment, there will be one classroom server and the students will have workstations named using consecutive numbers in place of the* xx *and* yy *variables. In a virtual lab environment, each student will have three virtual machines, named RWDC01, NYC-CL01, and NYC-CL02.*

In addition to the computers, you will also require the software listed in Table 12-2 to complete Lab 12.

Table 12-2
Software required for Lab 12

Software	*Location*
Lab 12 student worksheet	Lab12_worksheet.rtf (provided by instructor)

Working with Lab Worksheets

Each lab in this manual requires that you answer questions, make screen shots, and perform other activities that you will document on a worksheet named for the lab, such as Lab12_worksheet.rtf. Your instructor will provide you with access to the worksheets. It is recommended that you use a USB flash drive to store your worksheets, so you can submit them to your instructor for review. As you perform the exercises in each lab, open the appropriate worksheet file using WordPad, fill in the required information, and save the file to your flash drive.

SCENARIO

You are a Windows 7 technical specialist for Contoso Ltd. a company with workstations in a variety of different environments including multiple clients running Windows 7. To make sure the clients remain secure, you need to ensure that each client has the newest Windows updates and configure the Windows Firewall to protect each system.

After completing this lab, you will be able to:

- Configure Windows Firewall
- Use Windows Defender
- Encrypt files with Encrypting File System and BitLocker

Estimated lab time: 60 minutes

Exercise 12.1	Configuring Windows Firewall
Overview	The Windows Firewall is used to protect your computer, especially if you are connected to a public network. However, any firewall can also block packets, which may cause an application or service to fail. Therefore, you will need to know how to configure Windows firewall and troubleshoot as needed.
Completion time	10 minutes

1. Click the **Start** button and open the **Control Panel**.
2. Click **System and Security** followed by clicking **Windows Firewall**.
3. Click the **Turn Windows Firewall on or off** option.

Question 1	*For which profiles is the Windows Firewall enabled?*

4. Click the **Back** button.
5. Click the **Allow a program or feature through Windows Firewall** option.
6. Click the **Allow Another program** button.
7. Select **Internet Explorer** and click the **Add** button.
8. Click the **OK** button.
9. Click the **Advanced settings** option.

Question 2	*What program is open now?*

10. Click the **Inbound Rules** option in the left pane.
11. Click the **New Rule** option.
12. Select the **Port** option and click the **Next** button.
13. Specify TCP port **80** and **443** (specified as 80, 443) and click the **Next** button.
14. With the *Allow the connection* option selected, click the **Next** button.

15. When it asks which profiles to enable this rule for, keep all selected and click the **Next** button.

16. For the name, specify **Web Interface** and click the **Finish** button.

17. Close the Windows Firewall.

Exercise 12.2	Using Windows Defender
Overview	It is highly recommended that you use an antivirus package. Therefore, Contoso Ltd. has decided to investigate different software packages that will be used to protect the company computers. You decide to look at Windows Defender to see what protection it has to offer. Although many different antivirus software packages exist, you will find that many of the settings in Windows Defender are similar to other antivirus software settings.
Completion time	15 minutes

1. Click the **Start** button and search for *Windows Defender*. When found under the *Control Panel*, click **Windows Defender**.

2. If Windows Defender is turned off, you will get a message saying, "This program is turned off." If this message appears, click the **click here to turn it on** link.

3. For any antivirus program to be effective, it must be up-to-date. Therefore, if you are connected to the Internet, click the **Check for updates now** button.

4. Open the **Scan** menu and click **Quick Scan**. A quick scan will look for the most common places that viruses exist.

5. If it finds potential unwanted items, click the **Review detected items** link. Review the alert box and click the **Clean system** button. When the items have been cleaned, click the **Close** button.

6. Click the **Tools** option and click **Quarantined Items**. If an item was found to be malware and the software was configured to quarantine the malware instead of deleting it, it would be found here.

7. Click the **Tools** option again.

8. Click **Options**.

9. To perform a quick scan on a regular basis, make sure the following settings are set:

   - *Automatically scan my computer (recommended option)* is selected
   - *Frequency* is set to **Daily**
   - *Approximate time* is set to **2:00 AM**

- *Type* is set to **Quick scan**
- *Check for updated definitions before scanning* option is selected
- *Run a scan only when system is idle* option is selected

10. Scanning will only find malware while it is actually scanning. To protect your system all the time, you need to enable real-time protection so that if you access a file that contains malware that Windows Defender can identify, you will be notified immediately. To enable real-time protection, select the **Real-time protection** option.
11. Make sure the following options are enabled:
    - *Use real-time protection (recommended)*
    - *Scan downloaded files and attachments*
    - *Scan programs that run on my computer*
12. Sometimes, antivirus software can cause problems with certain applications. Therefore, you may need to exclude certain files from being scanned. To specify an individual file or folder, click the **Excluded files and folders** option.
13. To exclude a file type, click the **Excluded File types** option. To exclude all files with a .dbf file name extension, type ***.dbf** in the empty text box and click the **Add** button.
14. Click the **Advanced** option. The Advanced options allow you to specify if you want it to scan archive files, emails and removable drives.
15. Click the **Save** button.
16. Close Windows Defender.

Exercise 12.3	Looking at Encrypting File System
Overview	Within Contoso Ltd. there are files that users work with that are considered "Top Secret." As a network administrator, you have been asked to make these files as secure as possible. Therefore, you decide to investigate encrypting these files with Encrypting File System (EFS).
Completion time	20 minutes

1. Create a folder called **C:\EFS**.
2. Open the **EFS** folder.
3. Right-click the **EFS** folder and select **New** followed by **Text document**. Type **Test** and press the **Enter** key.

4. Right-click the file and select **Properties** to display the *Properties* dialog box.

5. Click the **Advanced** button.

6. Select the **Encrypt contents to secure data** option and click the **OK** button. Click the **OK** button to close the *Properties* dialog box.

7. When the Encryption warning appears, read the message. With the **Apply changes to this folder, subfolders and file** option selected, click the **OK** button.

8. Try to open the text file and type your name into the text file. Then save the file and close Notepad.

9. Log off as administrator and log in as local **TestUser** account with the *password* of **Password01**.

10. Try to access the text file in the EFS.

Question 3	*What color was the EFS folder?*

Question 4	*Were you able to access the encrypted file?*

11. Log off and log back in as **administrator** with the password of **Password01**.

12. Click the **Start** button and then click **Control Panel**. Then click **User Accounts** followed by clicking **User Accounts** again.

13. In the left pane, click the **Manage Your File Encryption Certificates** option.

14. When the *Encrypting File System Wizard* starts, click the **Next** button.

15. On the *Select Or Create A File Encryption Certificate* page, click **Next**.

16. On the *Back Up The Certificate And Key* page, click **Browse** and select the **Documents** folder. Type **EFS-cert-backup.pfx** for the filename. Click **Save**.

17. When it asks for the password, type **Password01** as needed and then click the **Next** button. Assigning a password to a file provides an extra layer of protection in case someone gets a hold of your EFS certificate backup files.

18. When it asks if you want to update your previously encrypted file, click the **Next** button.

19. Read the warning on the screen. On the *Encrypting File System* page, click **Close**.

20. Verify that the EFS-cert-backup.pfx file is in the Documents folder. In real life, you should then store the .pfx file in a safe place such as a spare drive or USB flash drive.

21. Click the **Start** button, and type **mmc** in the *Search programs and files* text box. If it asks if you are sure you want to open up MMC, click the **Yes** button.

22. Open the **File** menu and click **Add/Remove Snap-in.**

23. Double-click **Certificates**. With *My User Account* selected, click **Finish.**

24. Click **OK** to close the *Add or Remove Snap-ins* dialog box.

25. Expand *Certificates*, expand *Personal*, and then select **Certificates.**

26. Right-click **your EFS certificate**, and then click **Delete**. When it asks if you want to delete the certificate, click **Yes**.

27. Since EFS is still cached in memory, log off and then log back in as administrator.

28. Open the **C:\EFS** folder and try to open the **Test document**.

Question 5	*Were you able to access the encrypted file?*

29. Open your **Documents** folder.

30. Double-click the **EFS-cert-backup.pfx** file to start the *Certificate Import Wizard.* Click the **Next** button.

31. When it asks which file to import, click the **Next** button.

32. When it asks for the password, type **Password01**. Select the **Make this key as exportable** option. Click the **Next** button.

33. On the *Certificate Store* page, click **Next.**

34. When the wizard is complete, click the **Finish** button.

35. When the import is finished, click the **OK** button.

36. Go back to the **C:\EFS** folder and try to open the **Test document**.

Question 6	*Were you able to access the encrypted file?*

Exercise 12.4	Using BitLocker
Overview	In addition to investigating power settings, your director wants you to examine the BitLocker feature included in Windows 7. For your first experiment, you will use BitLocker to encrypt an external drive connected to your workstation using a password. Following that, you will then decrypt the drive.
Completion time	15 minutes

1. Log in as **administrator** with the password of ***Pa$$w0rd***.

2. Connect a USB flash drive to your system. If a USB flash drive is not available, use *Computer Management > Disk Management* to create a 10 GB NTFS partition.

Question 7	*Which edition(s) of Windows 7 supports BitLocker ToGo?*

3. Right-click the **drive that you are going to encrypt with BitLocker** and select **Turn On BitLocker**. The *BitLocker wizard* opens.

4. Enable the **Use a password to unlock the drive** and type **Password01** for the password. Click the **Next** button.

5. Click the **Save the recovery key to a file** option. When it asks to save it in the Documents library, click the **Save** button. Of course, similar to EFS, you want to save this file to a safe place. You should not save the file to your computer and should not use the flash drive that you are encrypting.

6. When it asks if you are ready to encrypt this drive, click the **Start Encrypting** button. Encrypting your drive will take several minutes depending on the size of the drive.

7. The encryption is complete when a confirmation dialog box opens. Click the **Close** button.

8. Click the **Start** button and click **Computers**.

Question 8	*What icon is used to show that the drive is encrypted?*

9. Give the USB drive to your partner and insert the drive into a USB port. When it asks for the password, type **Password01** and click **Unlock**. Then open **Computer** and double-click on the **encrypted drive**. Although it will not be used in this exercise, note that there is an *Automatically unlock the drive on this computer* option.

10. Remove the USB drive from your partner's computer and put it back into your system. When it asks for the password, type **Password01** and click **Unlock**.

11. Click the **Start** button and open the **Control Panel**. The *Control Panel* window appears.

12. Click **System and Security** and then click **BitLocker Drive Encryption**. The *BitLocker Drive Encryption control panel* appears.

13. Click the **Turn On BitLocker** link for your USB drive. The *BitLocker Drive Encryption Wizard* appears, displaying the *Choose how you want to unlock this drive* page.

14. To remove encryption, click the **Turn Off BitLocker** for the encrypted drive. Then click **Decrypt Drive**. This will take a couple of minutes depending on the size of the drive.

15. When the decryption is complete as indicated by a completion dialog box, click the **Close** button.

16. Close the BitLocker Drive Encryption control panel and log off of the workstation.

APPENDIX: LAB SETUP GUIDE

The Windows 7, Enterprise Desktop Support Technician title of the Microsoft Official Academic Course (MOAC) series includes two books: a textbook and a lab manual. The exercises in the lab manual are designed either for a virtual machine environment or for classroom use under the supervision of an instructor or lab aide. In an academic setting, the computer lab might be used by a variety of classes each day, so you must plan your setup procedure accordingly. For example, consider automating the classroom setup procedure and using removable hard disks in the classroom. You can use the automated setup procedure to rapidly configure the classroom environment, and remove the fixed disks after teaching this class each day.

LAB CONFIGURATION

This course should be taught in a lab containing networked computers where students can develop their skills through hands-on experience with Microsoft Windows 7. The exercises in the lab manual require the computers to be installed and configured in a specific manner. Failure to adhere to the setup instructions in this document can produce unanticipated results when the students perform the exercises.

The lab configuration consists of a single server running Microsoft Windows Server 2008 R2 Enterprise and a number of workstations. In the first lab, the students will install Windows 7 Enterprise.

The lab computers are located on an isolated network, configured as an Active Directory Domain Services (AD DS) domain separate from the rest of the school or organization network. The lab server functions as an Active Directory Domain Services domain controller and performs a number of other roles at various times throughout the course.

The lab uses the following information for the AD DS and server configuration:

- Active Directory Domain Services domain name: contoso.com
- Computer name: RWDC01
- Fully qualified domain name (FQDN): rwdc01.contoso.com

This document includes a setup procedure that configures the server to provide all of the infrastructure services required throughout the course. Once you have completed the initial setup, no further modifications to the lab server should be necessary.

The workstations in the lab are named NYC-CL*xx*, where *xx* is a unique number assigned to each computer. Each workstation will be a member of the contoso.com domain throughout most of the exercises, and also have a local administrative account called Student.

NOTE	*For the purposes of this lab, all server and workstation passwords, for user accounts and other purposes, will be set to* ***Pa$$w0rd****. This is obviously not a secure practice in a real-world situation, and instructors should remind students of this at the outset.*

Some of the lab exercises have dependencies on previous exercises, as noted in the lab manual and the instructor notes for each exercise. Students should perform the lab exercises in order and may have to complete any exercises they have missed due to absence before proceeding to the next lab.

Server Requirements

The computer running Windows Server 2008 R2 in the classroom requires the following hardware and software:

Hardware Requirements

- Minimum: 1.5 GHz x64 processor
- Minimum: 1 GB RAM (2 GB recommended)
- Minimum: 80 GB disk drive
- DVD drive
- Network interface adapter
- Wireless adapter
- Minimum: Super VGA (1024 x 768) display
- Keyboard
- Mouse

Software Requirements

All of the software listed here is required for this course:

- **Microsoft Windows Server 2008 R2 Enterprise**: The evaluation edition available as a free download from Microsoft's website at http://www.microsoft.com/windowsserver2008/en/us/trial-software.aspx
- **Remote Server Administration Tools for Windows 7**: Download x86fre_GRMRSAT_MSU.msu and/or amd64fre_GRMRSATX_MSU.msu from http://www.microsoft.com/downloads/details.aspx?displaylang=en& FamilyID=7d2f6ad7-656b-4313-a005-4e344e43997d
- Windows 7 Enterprise edition
- Windows XP Mode (WindowsXPMode_en-us.exe), Windows Virtual PC (Windows6.1-KB977206-x64.exe), and Windows XP Mode update (Windows6.1-KB958559-x64.exe). Download all from http://www.microsoft.com/windows/virtual-pc/download.aspx
- Flashmath for Windows 95, a freeware program, which can be downloaded from http://www.myfreewares.com/software-145420-flashmath-for-windows-95-free-download.html
- Memalloc.exe, which can be downloaded from http://www.soft.tahionic.com/download-memalloc/index.html
- Search for and download Microsoft Application Verifier from the Microsoft website. Currently, it is located at http://www.microsoft.com/downloads/en/details.aspx?familyid=c4a25ab9-649d-4a1b-b4a7-c9d8b095df18&displaylang=en
- Search for and download Microsoft Application Compatibility Toolkit 5.6 from the Microsoft website. Currently, it is located at http://www.microsoft.com/downloads/en/details.aspx?familyid=24da89e9-b581-47b0-b45e-492dd6da2971&displaylang=en

> **NOTE** *This list includes both 32- and 64-bit versions of the software products, where available. If all of your workstations use the same processor platform, you need to download one of the versions.*

With the exception of the Windows Server 2008 R2 operating system itself, the software products listed here do not have to be installed on the server. You must, however, download them and make them available to the workstation on a server share. The students will install each of these products at various points in the course.

Workstation Requirements

Each workstation requires the following hardware and software:

Hardware Requirements

- Minimum: 1 GHz 32-bit (x86) or 64-bit (x64) processor
- Minimum: 1 GB RAM (32-bit) / 2 GB RAM (64-bit)
- Minimum: 80 GB hard drive
- DVD drive
- Network interface adapter
- Network Adapter
- Minimum: Super VGA (1024 x 768) display
- Keyboard
- Mouse
- USB flash drive

Software Requirements

All of the software listed here is required for the course:

- Windows 7 Enterprise edition

> **NOTE** *Each of the student workstations can run either the 32- or 64-bit version of Windows as long as the computer has the appropriate hardware for the operating system and you provide each workstation with the additional software it needs in the version for the appropriate platform.*

SERVER SETUP INSTRUCTIONS

Before you begin, do the following:

- Read this entire document.
- Make sure you have the installation disks for Microsoft Windows Server 2008 R2 and Microsoft Windows 7.

Installing the Lab Server

Overview	Using the following procedure, install Windows Server 2008 R2 on RWDC01. This procedure assumes that you are performing a clean installation of the Windows Server 2008 R2 Enterprise evaluation edition, and that, if you have downloaded an image file, you have already burned it to a DVD-ROM disk.
Completion time	20 minutes

> NOTE
> *By performing the following setup instructions, your computer's hard disks will be repartitioned and reformatted. You will lose all existing data on these systems.*

1. Turn the computer on and insert the Windows Server 2008 R2 installation DVD into the drive.
2. Press any key, if necessary, to boot from the DVD-ROM disk. The Setup program loads, and the Install Windows window appears.
3. Modify the *Language to install, Time and currency format*, and *Keyboard or input method* settings, if necessary, and click Next.
4. Click Install Now. The *Select the operating system you want to install* page appears.
5. Select Windows Server 2008 R2 Enterprise (Full Installation) and click Next. The *Please read the license terms page* appears.
6. Select the *I accept the license terms* check box and click Next. The *Which type of installation do you want?* page appears.
7. Click *Custom (advanced)*. The *Where do you want to install Windows?* page appears.

> NOTE
> *If there are existing partitions on the computer's hard disk, select each one in turn and delete it before proceeding.*

8. Select Disk 0 Unallocated Space and click Next. The Installing Windows page appears, indicating the progress of the Setup program as it installs the operating system. After the installation completes and the computer restarts, a message appears stating that *The user's password must be changed before logging on the first time.*
9. Click OK. A Windows logon screen appears.
10. In the *New password* and *Confirm Password* text boxes, type **Pa$$w0rd** and click the right-arrow button. A message appears stating that *Your password has been changed.*

11. Click OK. The logon process completes, and the Initial Configuration Tasks window appears.

    Once the installation process is finished, you must complete the following tasks to configure the server and install the necessary roles to support the student workstations.

Completing Initial Server Configuration Tasks

Overview	Complete the following configuration tasks before you install Active Directory Domain Services or any other roles on the server.
Completion time	10 minutes

Configuring Date and Time Settings

1. In the Initial Configuration Tasks window, click *Set time zone*. The Date and Time dialog box appears.

2. If the time and/or date shown in the dialog box are not correct, click *Change date and time* and, in the Date and Time Settings dialog box, set the correct date and time and click OK.

3. If the time zone is not correct for your location, click *Change time zone* and, in the Time Zone Settings dialog box, set the correct time zone and click OK.

Configuring TCP/IP Settings

1. In the Initial Configuration Tasks window, click Configure networking. The Network Connections window appears.

2. Right-click the Local Area Connection icon and, from the context menu, select Properties. The Local Area Connection Properties sheet appears.

3. Select Internet Protocol Version 4 (TCP/IPv4) and click Properties. The Internet Protocol Version 4 (TCP/IPv4) Properties sheet appears.

4. Select the *Use the following IP address* option and configure the following settings:

    - IP address: 10.10.0.2
    - Subnet mask: 255.255.255.0
    - Default gateway: Leave blank
    - Preferred DNS server: 10.10.0.2
    - Alternate DNS server: Leave blank

Because you do not have a default gateway, you will not be able to connect to the Internet. Ask your lab administrator if you should configure a default gateway.

5. Click OK to close the Internet Protocol Version 4 (TCP/IPv4) Properties sheet.

6. Click Close to close the Local Area Connection Properties sheet.

7. Close the Network Connections window.

Naming the Server

1. In the Initial Configuration Tasks window, click Provide computer name and domain. The System Properties sheet appears.

2. Click Change. The Computer Name/Domain Changes dialog box appears.

3. In the *Computer name* text box, type **RWDC01** and click OK.

4. A Computer Name/Domain Changes message box appears, stating that you must restart the computer.

5. Click OK.

6. Click Close to close the System Properties dialog box. A Microsoft Windows message box appears, instructing you to restart the computer.

7. Click Restart Now. The system restarts.

Installing Server Roles

Overview	After configuring the Windows server, you can begin to install the server roles needed to support the student workstation, as described in the following sections.
Completion time	45 minutes

Installing Active Directory Domain Services

1. Log on to the server using the **Administrator** account and the password **Pa$$w0rd**. The Initial Configuration Tasks window appears.

2. Under Customize This Server, click *Add roles*. The Add Roles Wizard appears.

3. Click Next to bypass the Before You Begin page. The Select Server Roles page appears.

4. Select the Active Directory Domain Services check box. The *Add features required for Active Directory Domain Services?* dialog box appears.

5. Click Add Required Features. Then click Next. The Introduction to Active Directory Domain Services page appears.

6. Click Next. The Confirm Installation Selections page appears.

7. Click Install. The Installation Results page appears.

8. Click *Close this wizard and launch the Active Directory Domain Services Installation Wizard (dcpromo.exe)*. The Active Directory Domain Services Installation Wizard appears.

9. Click Next to bypass the Welcome page. The Operating System Compatibility page appears.

10. Click Next. The Choose a Deployment Configuration page appears.

11. Select the *Create a new domain in a new forest* option and click Next. The Name the Forest Root Domain page appears.

12. In the *FWDN of the forest root domain* text box, type **contoso.com** and click Next. The Set Forest Functional Level page appears.

13. In the *Forest functional level* drop-down list, select Windows Server 2008 R2 and click Next. The Additional Domain Controller options page appears.

14. Click Next. An Active Directory Domain Services Installation Wizard message box appears.

15. Click Yes. The Location for Database, Log Files, and SYSVOL page appears.

16. Click Next. The Directory Services Restore Mode Administrator Password page appears.

17. In the Password and Confirm Password text boxes, type **Pa$$w0rd** and click Next. The Summary page appears.

18. Click Next. The wizard installs Active Directory Domain Services. The Completing the Active Directory Domain Services Installation Wizard page appears.

19. Click Finish. Then click Restart Now. The computer restarts.

Installing Active Directory Certificate Services

1. Log on to the server using the **Administrator** account and the password **Pa$$w0rd**. The Initial Configuration Tasks window appears.

2. Under Customize This Server, click *Add roles*. The Add Roles Wizard appears.

3. Click Next to bypass the Before You Begin page. The Select Server Roles page appears.

4. Select the Active Directory Certificate Services check box and click Next. The Introduction to Active Directory Certificate Services page appears.

5. Click Next. The Select Role Services page appears.

6. Select the Certification Authority Web Enrollment check box. The *Add role services and features required for Certification Authority Web Enrollment?* dialog box appears.

7. Click Add Required Role Services. Then click Next. The *Specify Setup Type* page appears.

8. Click Next to accept the default Enterprise option. The *Specify CA Type* page appears.

9. Click Next to accept the default Root CA option. The *Set Up Private Key* page appears.

10. Click Next to accept the default settings. The *Configure Cryptography for CA* page appears.

11. Click Next to accept the default settings. The *Configure CA Name* page appears.

12. Click Next to accept the default settings. The *Set Validity Period* page appears.

13. Click Next to accept the default settings. The *Configure Certificate Database* page appears.

14. Click Next to accept the default settings. The *Web Server (IIS)* page appears.

15. Click Next. The *Select Role Services* page appears.

16. Click Next to accept the default settings. The *Confirm Installation Selections* page appears.

17. Click Install. The wizard installs the selected role services and the *Installation Results* page appears.

18. Click Close.

Installing DHCP Server

1. In the Initial Configuration Tasks window, under Customize This Server, click *Add roles*. The Add Roles Wizard appears.

2. Click Next to bypass the Before You Begin page. The *Select Server Roles* page appears.

3. Select the DHCP Server check box and click Next. The *Introduction to DHCP Server* page appears.

4. Click Next. The *Select Network Connection Bindings* page appears.

5. Click Next to accept the default settings. The *Specify IPv4 DNS Server Settings* page appears.

6. Click Next to accept the default settings. The *Specify IPv4 WINS Server Settings* page appears.

7. Click Next to accept the default settings. The *Add or Edit DHCP Scopes* page appears.

8. Click Add. The *Add Scope* dialog box appears.

9. Complete the fields in the dialog box using the following values and click OK:

   - Scope name: contoso.com
   - Starting IP address: 10.10.0.100
   - Ending IP address: 10.10.0.199
   - Subnet mask: 255.0.0.0
   - Default gateway (optional): Leave blank

10. Click Next. The *Configure DHCPv6 Stateless Mode* page appears.

11. Click Next to accept the default settings. The *Specify IPv6 DNS Server Settings* page appears.

12. Click Next to accept the default settings. The *Authorize DHCP Server* page appears.

13. Click Next to accept the default settings. The *Confirm Installation Selections* page appears.

14. Click Install. The wizard installs the role and the *Installation Results* page appears.

15. Click Close.

Installing Routing and Remote Access

1. In the Initial Configuration Tasks window, under Customize This Server, click *Add roles*. The Add Roles Wizard appears.

2. Click Next to bypass the Before You Begin page. The *Select Server Roles* page appears.

3. Select the *Network Policy and Access Services* check box and click Next. The *Introduction to Network Policy and Access Services* page appears.

4. Click Next. The *Select Role Services* page appears.

5. Select the *Routing and Remote Access Services* check box and click Next. The *Confirm Installation selections* page appears.

6. Click Install. The *Installation Results* page appears.
7. Click Close.
8. Click Start. Then click Administrative Tools > Routing and Remote Access. The Routing and Remote Access console appears.
9. Right-click the RWDC01 (local) node and, from the context menu, select Configure and Enable Routing and Remote Access. The Routing and Remote Access Server Setup Wizard appears.
10. Click Next to bypass the Welcome page. The *Configuration* page appears.
11. Select the *Custom configuration* option and click Next. The *Custom Configuration* page appears.
12. Select the *VPN access* check box and click Next. The Completing the Routing and Remote Access Server Setup Wizard page appears.
13. Click Finish. A *Routing and Remote Access* message box appears.
14. Click *Start service*. The wizard configures Routing and Remote Access and starts the service.
15. Close the Routing and Remote Access console.

Preparing the Server File System

Overview	After configuring the Windows server, you can begin to install the server roles needed to support the student workstation, as described in the following sections.
Completion time	45 minutes

1. Download all of the free software products listed in the Software Requirements section, earlier in this document.
2. On the RWDC01 server, open Windows Explorer and create a new folder on the C: drive called **downloads**.
3. Share the downloads folder using the name **downloads**.
4. Assign the Allow Full Control share permission to the Everyone special identity.
5. Copy the following to the c:\download folder:
   - **Remote Server Administration Tools for Windows 7**: Download from x86fre_GRMRSAT_MSU.msu and/or amd64fre_GRMRSATX_MSU.msu
   - Windows XP Mode (WindowsXPMode_en-us.exe), Windows Virtual PC (Windows6.1-KB977206-x64.exe), and Windows XP Mode update (Windows6.1-KB958559-x64.exe).

- MemAlloc.exe from http://www.soft.tahionic.com/download-memalloc/index.html
- Download and unzip the Flashmath for Windows 95 (a freeware program) files into the flmath95 folder in the downloads folder. Flashmath can be downloaded from http://www.myfreewares.com/software-145420-flashmath-for-windows-95-free-download.html
- Search for and download Microsoft Application Verifier from the Microsoft website. Currently, it is located at http://www.microsoft.com/downloads/en/details.aspx?familyid=c4a25ab9-649d-4a1b-b4a7-c9d8b095df18&displaylang=en
- Search for and download Microsoft Application Compatibility Toolkit 5.6 from the Microsoft website. Currently, it is located at http://www.microsoft.com/downloads/en/details.aspx?familyid=24da89e9-b581-47b0-b45e-492dd6da2971&displaylang=en
- Download the installation files for the newest version of Adobe Acrobat reader

6. Create a folder called win7ent in the c:\download folder and copy the Windows 7 installation files into the win7ent folder.

Exercise 3 Setup

1. Before the students start Exercise 3, open the Default Domain Policy and change the (Computer Configuration>Windows Settings> Account Policies>Account Lockout Policy) Account Lockout Policy to the following settings:
   - Account lockout duration: 30 Minutes
   - Account lockout threshold: 3 invalid logon Attempts
   - Reset account lockout counter after: 30 Minutes
2. At the end of class, disable Account Lockout Policy.

Exercise 4 Setup

1. Configure the wireless access point with a SSID of Contoso01 and enable WPA2-Personal with the Pa$$w0rd security key.

WORKSTATION SETUP INSTRUCTIONS

During the first lab, the students will be performing a clean install of Windows 7 Enterprise. If the students are using physical computers, students will need to have installation DVDs of Windows 7. If the students are using virtual computers, you will need to place copies of the installation ISOs on their hard drives so that the students can mount the ISO image as their DVD disk.